T0271429

DIGITIZATION AND CULTURE IN VIETNAM

The accessibility of cultural resources via digital platforms is empowering Vietnamese cultural professionals to promote their culture to local and international audiences.

This shortform book investigates the significance of digitization in Vietnamese culture, illuminating how cultural professionals are empowered through the process of digitization. The author shows how digitization is not an entirely comprehensive, ethical, or sustainable solution for the cultural sector in Vietnam, as cultural professionals working at nonprofit art spaces and artists experience both opportunities and challenges in digitizing art and culture.

Drawing on new interviews with cultural professionals working in the cultural sector in Vietnam, the book will be of interest to scholars and reflective practitioners involved with the cultural and creative industries in South East Asia and globally.

Emma Duester is an Associate professor at the Institute of Cultural and Creative Industry, Shanghai Jiao Tong University, Shanghai, China. She has published widely on the culture sector, mobilities, transnational communication, and digitization of culture in Europe and Vietnam. This book is the result of a funded research project at RMIT University Vietnam, carried out between 2020 and 2021.

Routledge Focus on the Global Creative Economy
Series Editor: Aleksandar Brkić, Goldsmiths, University of London, UK

This innovative Shortform book series aims to provoke and inspire new ways of thinking, new interpretations, emerging research, and insights from different fields. In rethinking the relationship of creative economies and societies beyond the traditional frameworks, the series is intentionally inclusive. Featuring diverse voices from around the world, books in the series bridge scholarship and practice across arts and cultural management, the creative industries and the global creative economy.

Cultural Mediation for Museums
Driving Audience Engagement
Edited by Michela Addis, Isabella de Stefano and Valeria Guerrisi

Rethinking Cultural Centers
A Nordic Perspective on Multipurpose Cultural Organizations
Tomas Järvinen

Curating, Interpretation and Museums
When Attitude Becomes Form
Sylvia Lahav

Contemporary Exhibition-Making and Management
Curating IMT Gallery as a Hybrid Space
Mark Rohtmaa-Jackson

Digitization and Culture in Vietnam
Emma Duester

For more information about this series, please visit: www.routledge.com/Routledge-Focus-on-the-Global-Creative-Economy/book-series/RFGCE

Digitization and Culture
in Vietnam

Emma Duester

Routledge
Taylor & Francis Group

LONDON AND NEW YORK

First published 2023
by Routledge
4 Park Square, Milton Park, Abingdon, Oxon OX14 4RN

and by Routledge
605 Third Avenue, New York, NY 10158

Routledge is an imprint of the Taylor & Francis Group, an informa business

© 2023 Emma Duester

The right of Emma Duester to be identified as author of this work has
been asserted in accordance with sections 77 and 78 of the Copyright,
Designs and Patents Act 1988.

British Library Cataloguing-in-Publication Data
A catalogue record for this book is available from the British Library

Library of Congress Cataloging-in-Publication Data
A catalog record has been requested for this book

ISBN: 978-1-032-40376-2 (hbk)
ISBN: 978-1-032-40377-9 (pbk)
ISBN: 978-1-003-35279-2 (ebk)

DOI: 10.4324/9781003352792

Typeset in Times New Roman
by codeMantra

Contents

Acknowledgements

This book comes from a research project that started in 2020. I would like to thank my research team who helped with the project.

I would like to thank Ms. Michal Teague, for her inspiration and for making things that seemed impossible possible.

I would like to thank Dr. Abdul Rohman and my research assistant Ms. Thoa Mai Thi Tran for collecting some of the literature and for carrying out some of the interviews in Vietnamese.

This project was funded by RMIT University from January 2020 until March 2022, so I would like to thank the university for making this project possible and for allowing it to continue even during the Covid-19 pandemic.

Introduction

The increasing use of digital technologies has brought significant transformation to the culture sector. It has transformed the work practices of cultural professionals and has increased the diversity and quality of art experiences and events online. This digital transition has opened up new opportunities as well as challenges. Cultural professionals can create new types of digital content and connect to new audiences in a variety of ways. However, there are also new pressures to keep up with these technological changes in order to meet audience demands and reach ever more digitally savvy audiences.

While there is a common global digital transition in the cultural sector, there are also aspects that are different around the world. Developments in digital transition are happening at different paces and rates, as the route, pace, and motive of digitization are diverse and vary in different parts of the world. Moreover, some places are not yet documented and do not have many available resources online. This is due to the varying degrees of ability to adopt digital technologies, varying amounts of inclusion in the global discourse on art and culture, and an imbalance in representation of art and culture online (that are more swayed towards Western, developed nations). Therefore, digitization and digital display on digital platforms can allow increased inclusion of more non-Western aesthetic perspectives and help to address the current inequalities in the amount of accessible content online as well as the disparities in access to high-quality technical equipment, staff, and funding, as well as disparities in the control of production and circulation of cultural content online.

Global transition towards digitization is affecting the cultural sector in the Global South, in terms of pressure to digitize at a fast pace but often without sufficient human, technical, and financial resources. Yet, digitization and accessibility are critical for developing countries to develop their cultural industry and economy, and importance lies in giving access to cultural content online and increasing the amount of available, accessible resources online. Developing countries in the Global South do not have the same level of access to high-quality digital technologies or enough skilled personnel to digitize sufficiently. Today, there is still a disparity globally in the amount of accessible resources online about art and culture. In response to these concerns, this

DOI: 10.4324/9781003352792-1

book will identify how Vietnam is not equally represented online in terms of the number of available resources. This book is therefore important for raising awareness on these issues, such as there being not enough available digital resources on contemporary Vietnamese art and culture, as well as being an important resource about Vietnamese contemporary art and culture. Hence, this book will become one such accessible resource or, at least, highlight how digital culture (i.e. the creation and curation of culture online) is being created in Vietnam on digital platforms and show how digital platforms can become spaces for professional, curated digital culture and a space where educators, researchers, students, and the general public can access available cultural resources.

It is important to include Vietnam in this discourse because this nation's cultural sector is currently going through the process of digital transition, with trials in virtual exhibitions, virtual and augmented reality technologies for art and culture content, and experimentation of new technologies to reignite traditional Vietnamese art styles. Moreover, the country's history and culture are germane to the current state and progress of digital transition, resulting in specific routes, modes, and approaches in the digitization and display process as well as with the creation of digital culture. Global forces and geopolitics also affect the nature of the routes towards digitization and display of cultural content in Vietnam today. As Feher et al. (2017) argue, different industries and regions have numerous and nuanced adaptations towards digitization.

Digitization processes in Vietnam are bound up with local, regional, and global forces. Thus, this book explores the affects of local, national, and global forces on digital culture in Vietnam. This will include investigation into the creation of digital culture through digitization practices and publication techniques today online. It will also include analysis of the challenges and opportunities faced by cultural professionals while going through this digital transition in the Global South. This book shows how our understanding of digitization can be strengthened by connecting to the cultural, geopolitical and economic, and historic contexts. It will show how digital culture is country-specific and time-specific but also reflective of the time-period and historical moment globally. Importantly, this assessment of what is happening in the local context will also be assessed in relation to what is happening in the cultural industries globally.

The overarching theme of this book pertains to the nexus between technology and culture. A great deal written about this comes from media studies (Deuze 2006; Gere 2002; Sadiku et al. 2017; Uzelac 2010) and from the technical side of digitization about coding and metadata (Astle and Miur 2002; Yilmaz and Celic 2011). As a result, more is needed on the intersection of technology and culture and the subsequent creation of digital culture. In addition, it is important to show how digital culture is essentially being created by individual cultural professionals and to shed light on their experiences going through this process of digital transition. Together, this book is about the creative and innovative uses of technology in the cultural sector by cultural professionals to create digital culture online. Cultural professionals (namely curators, art gallery directors, art space founders, and artists) are the producers, curators, and 'mediators' of contemporary digital culture, acting as an important source of access to and education about art and culture. This book is transdisciplinary, combining cultural studies, media studies, social media studies, arts and cultural sector studies, and technology and digital technology studies.

Digitization is the most recent mode of presenting culture online using digital technology. With digitization, cultural professionals can document a wide range of aspects of their work, including both the process and final product. The current technology of digitization can provide a new way of representing culture, create new meanings about culture, and reveal a new way of experiencing culture. Digitization has been developing and used more and more globally over the past few decades. The publication of digitized content onto digital platforms has been especially needed and developed during the Covid-19 pandemic. Digitization is the process of transferring materials (photographs, slides, and 3D objects) in a variety of environments into a format that can be viewed in a digital environment (Astle and Miur 2002). Digitization is a "conversion process of physical or analogue materials such as paper documents, photographs or graphical materials into an electronic environment or into images stored in electronic environment" (Yilmaz and Çelic 2011 118). However, this book presents it as more than its technical definition. Instead, this book focuses on the cultural side of digitization; it is seen here as a cultural practice and as an artform in itself. Hence, it is not only documenting culture. Instead, digitization can be seen as culture because it is a way of revealing ways of life, artefacts, and meanings digitally.

This digital transition in Vietnam is being done independently by the nongovernmental sector, including nonprofit art spaces, private (but not profitable) galleries, and independent artists.[1] Yet, they face the most amount of challenges, frictions, and pressures in digitization and have little human, technical, and financial resources in comparison with the state cultural sector. This is a do-it-yourself (DIY) digitization culture and community of practice, whereby individuals are doing it independently, on their own, sometimes having to learn and train themselves in digital skills. They have made developments and transitions themselves, independent of government support, as individual projects with funding from international councils. This is in contrast to digitization projects at state museums that use government budget.[2] This means nonprofit art spaces and independent artists have had to find available digital solutions to digitize and display for free and on commonly used platforms. Hence, free and popular social media platforms like Facebook provide a viable way to digitize art and culture and overcome challenges with lack of human, technical, and financial resources. Many of these challenges, with lack of human, technical, and financial resources, are common globally in the cultural sector. However, in Vietnam, these challenges are more acute and are also intersected by more hidden challenges, such as language, stereotypes, and geopolitics. This shows that the challenges faced in the digitization process are not only practical but also about much more deep-seated issues related to culture and history. Together, this book problematizes whether digitization can be a comprehensive solution for the cultural sector in Vietnam, as they face practical challenges in their work, as well as additional more hidden challenges, as well as the need for greater inclusion and access to the global community in art and culture, the ability to create their own image of contemporary culture, and control of the narrative on Vietnamese culture.

During and since the Covid-19 pandemic, the ability to access culture via online has become more important. However, differences in levels of access, quality, and amount of content available have become more visible, as the Covid-19 pandemic has exacerbated existing digital inequalities in terms of funding and resources in the cultural sector. As ICOM (2020) argues, "the crisis has highlighted some structural weaknesses in terms of resources and staff dedicated to digital activities and communication, and level of maturity of the content produced". Nonprofit art spaces and independent artists have been particularly negatively affected during the Covid-19 pandemic, with smaller teams, less available funding, or government stipends. This is commonplace amongst nonprofit organizations and, hence, is not only the case in Vietnam. While the effects of the Covid-19 pandemic have been widely documented on museums in Europe (ICOM 2020; NEMO 2020), there needs to be more discussion on nonprofit art spaces and independent artists in the Global South.

There is an emergent digital culture as a result of increasing amounts of available content online along with developments in use of digital platforms for publishing, exhibiting, and experiencing art and culture.[3] However, digital platforms that are owned by Western tech giants have a powerful role as gatekeepers, mediators of culture, in governing the creation, curation, and presentation of digital culture. In this, we must take into consideration the fact that the platforms' codes, algorithms, terms, and conditions are largely created in the West by the West. For example, digital platforms frame what we see and how we see content, the order and layout design it takes on the page, and the weight given to certain stories over others. As a result, we need to think about what role technology should play in presenting culture online. How are we disseminating culture through the use of technology? Hence, some consideration is needed on who controls and how they influence digital culture. This will allow the author to assess how far Vietnamese cultural professionals have control over the creation of their own content. On the one hand, digital transition and increasing use of digital platforms in the cultural sector can enable new types of content to be easily uploaded and published, knowledge to be easily and widely shared and disseminated, and more diversity of voices to participate in the online discourse on art and culture. However, the question remains as to whether this is creating more equal inclusion and meaningful access for cultural professionals in the Global South or if it is exacerbating already existing forms of digital cultural colonialism? [4] Also, how is culture communicated, curated, and presented when it goes online? How is culture shaped by the tech giants that own the platforms? How is the culture of practice of professionals changing due to technology and digital transition globally?

This book captures individual cultural professionals' thoughts about and actual experiences of challenges and opportunities *during the process* of digitization and digital transition. This is in contrast to existing studies that analyse this afterwards (for instance, Beene, Soito, and Kohl 2020; Caraffa et al. 2020) or studies that use examples from archives (Lischer-Katz 2020). This makes this book timely and innovative in documenting this unique moment in transition. The author has chosen to document this transition stage and to reflect on it in the moment. As a result, this book documents cultural professionals' digital transition, their process through this, and how they are currently increasingly digitally documenting their own process. It is about how this is being created and what challenges are affecting this process of creating culture online today and what opportunities there are with new technologies that enable people to create new meanings and new possibilities with content creation online. Hence, it is not only about transition in Vietnam but also about global digital transition in the cultural sector and about the changing relations between technology and culture globally and changing use of technology to present, in terms of portraying culture online. However, it should be noted here that as something is created, it is then discussed only afterwards, and discourse is created. Therefore, as digitization and the creation of digital culture are only just happening in Vietnam, there is not yet much commentary on this from a Vietnamese perspective; hence, this book hopes to be one such resource on this topic.

This book is distinct as it takes the perspective from individual cultural professionals, specifically independent artists and nonprofit art spaces, contrary to the more common perspective from large museums (vom Lehn and Heath 2005; Thomas and Mintz 1998), or the audience's virtual experiences (Peacock and Brownbill 2007; Soren 2005). This demonstrates a need for more in-depth analysis of interviews with smaller organisations and individual artists. This also demonstrates a need for more in-depth analysis on art spaces in developing countries in Asia. As a result, this rich data can provide a much more in-depth and comprehensive assessment of what is happening in the cultural sector through the process of digital transition and during the moment of an emergent digital culture in Vietnam. Documenting this during the process can help to highlight both the opportunities and challenges. It will achieve this by drawing on 30 interviews with cultural professionals working in the cultural sector in Vietnam.[5] Cultural professionals include curators, directors, and artists from non-for-profit art spaces, private (but not profitable) galleries, and artists – all of which are non-governmental (I refer to them as 'cultural professionals' from here on). When referring to 'cultural professionals' throughout the book, I am specifically referring to the 28 cultural professionals (founders/directors of nonprofit art spaces, private galleries, or independent artists). It is not necessarily representative of all cultural professionals because it is such a small number. Yet, it is still relevant and important because it focuses on these individuals and their experiences. This research took place during the Covid-19 pandemic, so some of the interview questions are about impacts of the Covid-19 pandemic on work and managing the shift to working fully online, but I also wanted it to go beyond just Covid, as these changes in digital transition were happening before Covid and reflect a much larger and longer-term cultural shift toward digital technology, so questions also relate to changes in the sector over a five-year timeframe. That said, answers will be affected by the time and context of being during the Covid-19 pandemic.

This book focuses on curators, directors, and artists from non-for-profit art spaces, private (but not profitable) galleries, and independent artists – all of which are non-governmental – in the Global South and their (in)ability to be included in and to influence the global discourse on art and culture. While digital technologies and platforms increasingly allow cultural professionals' voices to be heard and included, these technologies also provide new types of hurdles and barriers along with a new set of digital inequalities. It is vitally important to understand these issues to prevent further digital inequalities and a continued invisible-ising of certain cultures in the future. Even though technological advancements allow new content, knowledge, and more voices to participate in the online discourse on art and culture, the question remains as to whether this is creating equal inclusion and meaningful access or if it is simply just exacerbating already existing forms of digital cultural colonialism? This has become especially evident during the Covid-19 pandemic, which has highlighted and heightened inequalities in digital access and inclusion.

This analysis of Vietnam is positioned alongside a discussion of current developments in the cultural industries regionally and globally. Together, this demonstrates how digitization practices have become an increasingly central aspect of cultural professionals' work practices, which includes both new challenges and opportunities. It also demonstrates how, today, there is still a disparity globally in the amount of accessible resources online about art and culture. This book is therefore important in raising awareness on these issues as well as being an important resource about Vietnamese contemporary art and culture. This book will identify how Vietnam is not equally represented online in terms of the number of available resources. I hope that this book can become one such accessible resource, or at least highlight how digital culture (i.e. the creation and curation of culture online) is being created in Vietnam on social media and show how digital platforms like Facebook can be spaces for professional, curated digital culture and that educators, researchers, students and general public can now access these available resources. This book is therefore important in raising awareness on these issues of there being not enough available digital resources on contemporary Vietnamese art and culture as well as being an important resource about Vietnamese contemporary art and culture in order to fill the gap.

Before moving on, I would like to share a bit about myself. I moved to Vietnam in 2019 to take up a position at RMIT University, an English-language Australian University in Vietnam. As a British citizen who has lived and worked predominantly in Europe, I am careful about my complex position in talking and writing about Vietnam. Even though I have experience in working with the culture sector in Europe, the context and situation in South East Asia is different. I am aware that my viewpoint is influenced by my background. I have spent three and a half years immersed in the culture sector in Vietnam. I have worked closely with independent and state art institutions as well as with organizations such as UNESCO and Vietnam Institute of Culture and Arts Studies (VICAS). From this, I gained invaluable insight, knowledge, and understanding about the people and culture. This book blends my critical spirit with a love for the Vietnamese culture. This book is a way to highlight and showcase the voices of these cultural professionals. I hope that some changes can be made as a result of this publication, which sheds some light on current situation as well as future requirements and needs for culture sector development.

Chapter Outline

Chapter 1 provides an overview of digital transition and development of the cultural industries in Asia. It discusses national digitization strategies and projects in China, Japan, and South Korea. It also outlines national policies on digitization and the development of the creative industries in South East Asia. Alongside this, it discusses the development of the creative industries in Europe and the USA in order to provide context on how government as well as private funding and support are essential to the development of this sector and for digital transition. In particular, it discusses how use of digital platforms has increased and are now being harnessed for work in the cultural sector. With this, it will explore how developments in use of digital platforms have led to the formation of a more comprehensive digital culture. The chapter discusses the issues of digital colonialism, as Western tech giants have increasing amounts of power to create regulations and policies that do not necessarily 'fit' with values or ways of working and communicating in the Global South. However, this discussion is positioned alongside the opposing argument of digital empowerment, whereby populations in the Global South can be empowered by being able to participate and have their voices included. The chapter will engage with scholarship that strives to highlight the barriers in inclusion, including the issues of unequal power relations, neocolonialism, digital illiteracy, barriers to access, and the digital divide.

Chapter 2 discusses how digitization has become one of the central aspects of work for cultural professionals in the culture sector in Vietnam. Whilst the digitization of art and culture has been predominantly for archiving and preservation, cultural professionals are now developing innovative ways of publishing and displaying digitized content by using new digital technologies and digital platforms. This chapter explores this shift in the nature of work for cultural professionals and how this is starting to produce a digital culture. This chapter explores cultural professionals' developments in digitization practices. It also looks at the challenges they are facing in this work and how these challenges are impeding digital transition. The chapter explores the challenges in lack of human resources, technical resources, and funding as well as more hidden challenges with (mis)representation and lack of available resources online. It will also consider the ethics of digitization and what constitutes meaningful access as well as the motives for digitization. This chapter will engage with cultural commentators on Vietnamese culture industry and members of the cultural industry who have written about current trends in the art, design, and branding. For instance, as Dan (2018) comments, the 'cultural industry' is a new term for the economy and culture of Vietnam, only coming into use over the last three to five years. Cultural tourism is spearheading the cultural industry, as Vietnam is a country with a rich cultural tradition, with many World Heritage Sites and cultural legacies. However, this chapter will show how this can also be applied to contemporary art and culture in Vietnam. For instance, Tuan Le – a Vietnamese designer (2018, cited in Vincetera) – says Vietnam is now about design and creativity; many in Vietnam are now trying to break away from stereotypical images of hems and straw hats and provide more diversity to redefine the contemporary image of Vietnamese culture. Richard Streitmatter-Tran – a contemporary artist (cited in Vincetera 2018) also says this is happening with regard to the contemporary art scene in Vietnam. He comments on how in 2017 we saw many Vietnam-based artists exhibit in major exhibitions both abroad and locally, and how contemporary art is changing global perspectives on Vietnamese culture. Vietnam News (December 17th 2020) has commented on digital transition in Vietnam, saying that 2020 was the starting year for the national digital transformation and 2022 saw further digital transformation. They say 2022 was the first year of implementing new strategies on digital infrastructure, data, technology industry, and technology enterprise in Vietnam (Vietnam News, December 24, 2021).

Chapter 3 focuses on examples of how digital platforms are used by cultural professionals to disseminate Vietnamese art and culture. It explores how this is creating a digital culture that is presented and communicated by cultural professionals and artists. It analyses how different types of digital platforms are used to display art and culture, including virtual exhibitions, online workshops, AR apps, websites and social media. However, it also sheds light on the concerns with having to use foreign technology. This chapter focuses on the dominance of Facebook in Vietnam as it is the most popular digital platform amongst the general public and professionals working in the culture sector in Vietnam. While cultural professionals have harnessed a variety of digital platforms for the display and experience of art and culture, they also face issues with image quality, search engine optimization (SEO), dual language, platform policies, and algorithms that perpetuate biases towards commercial content. This is important to consider as it determines what kind of digital culture is produced and how it is shown.

Chapter 4 provides foresight on future prospects and concerns for Vietnam's culture sector. To do this, this chapter shares cultural professionals' visions for the future of the culture sector in Vietnam. This sheds light on the future needs and requirements for the sector that are needed for their ambitions to be possible. Their needs for the culture sector's digital development include enhancing and enforcing intellectual property (IP) protection and copyright laws, creating a national digital culture policy, and creating common standards and professionalism amidst a predominantly DIY culture of practice. It will also share their future ambitions, which can only be achieved after their requirements are met, including more cross-sector collaboration, international connections, commercializing artworks with the use of online platforms, sharing more diverse range of topics and viewpoints due to the democratic potential of digital platforms amidst censorship laws in Vietnam for physical exhibitions, and the creation of a national archive for *contemporary* Vietnamese art. This chapter will assess the future of Vietnamese professionals' digitization practices amidst continuing issues of access and inclusion. The chapter will finish by considering what might be the future for Vietnamese art and artistic practices, including prospects around hybrid digital-physical offerings and digital-born art.

Notes

1 Nonprofit art spaces, non-governmental art galleries, and independent artists are a relatively new concept in Vietnam. Through history, art and culture have been linked with the State and propaganda. Nonprofits only started to emerge in Vietnam after Doi Moi in 1986 (Sidel 1997). Doi Moi was a series of reforms that allowed for the shift to a market economy. Due to this relatively late introduction, nonprofits have suffered and still struggles with a lot of challenges and do not have a robust legal framework or support from national level. Also, they are still today quite unique vis-à-vis the more common state run museums and art centres across Vietnam. Even for nonprofit art spaces and independent artists, all exhibitions and events must be approved by the Government and physical premises for operating art spaces must be granted permission and a license from the Government.

2 The nonprofit art sector is dependent on international councils and embassies for funding, such as the British Council and Goethe Institute, which sponsor exhibitions and projects. For instance, an exhibition and project at *Heritage Space* entitled 'MAP: Month of Arts Practice' was sponsored by the Goethe Institute and the British Council funds projects such as 'Connections through Culture'. However, these councils and institutes are also nonprofit, so they have also been impacted by Covid-19 pandemic, resulting in less available funding. There was also no government funding for nonprofit organizations during the lockdown and closure of physical premises because they fell outside of the six eligible categories for funding. As Minh reports (Vincetera, 2nd April 2020), "The Vietnamese Government is poised

to adopt a US$2.6 billion relief package to help those most affected by the covid-19 pandemic that has waged devastation on the economy. The draft Resolution on Government's covid-19 support, presented on Wednesday at the regular cabinet meeting by the Minister of Planning and Investment Nguyễn Chí Dũng, mostly sets out cash payments during a three-month period starting April through June. According to the bill, there will be six groups of people who are eligible for the relief payments. Social policy beneficiaries and those who have rendered services to the State during the revolution and wards receiving merit payments will be given an additional VNĐ500,000 ($21.8) each month in April, May, and June." This is in contrast to government museums that received a stipend through Covid and are funded by government for all work and projects.

3 Digital culture is a new form of culture that is created and displayed via digital technologies. It also describes how technology and the internet are shaping the way people interact, communicate, and socialise today. It is not only a tool to help us with our lives in the physical world as it now is a part of our lives and the physical world in a hybrid physical-digital environment.

4 Digital cultural colonialism is the ability of Western online platforms and aggregators to represent the epistemologies of dominant communities, reforming the epistemologies of the world outside Western culture. Places outside Western culture have impression of less importance and acquire 'otherness' (Kizhner et al. 2020).

5 30 interviews were carried out between May 2020 and 2021 with cultural professionals, including curators, directors and artists from non-for-profit art spaces, private (but not profitable) galleries, and independent artists – all of which are nongovernmental. This was carried out during the Covid-19 pandemic and hence reflect the feelings of the people at this time and the current zeitgeist. However, we also asked about changes over a five-year period and developments over this time frame, which means it is not about only the pandemic timeframe. It is important to chart the changes happening in this sector during the past five years, as it has included the Covid-19 pandemic but yet it is important to note that change was happening prior to this, yet of course it helped to accelerate the digitization of culture: 14 nonprofits art organisations, three private (but not profitable) galleries, and 13 artists.

References

Astle, P. J., and A. Miur. 2002. "Digitization and Preservation in Public Libraries and Archives." *Journal of Librarianship and Information Science* 34(2): 67–79. https://doi.org/10.1177/096100060203400202. Search in Google Scholar

Beene, S., L. Soito, and L. Kohl. (2020) "Art Catalogs Unbound: Overcoming Challenges through Engagement." Art Documentation: *Journal of the Art Libraries Society of North America* 39(1): 24–43.

Caraffa, C., E. Pugh, T. Stuber, and L. Ruby. (2020). "PHAROS: A Digital Research Space for Photo Archives." *Art Libraries Journal* 45(1): 2–11. https://doi.org/10.1017/alj.2019.34

Dan, N. (2018) "Developing Vietnam's Cultural Industry." Asia Views. https://Asiaviews.net/developing-vietnams-cultural-industry

Deuze, M. (2006). "Participation, Remediation, Bricolage: Considering Principal Components of a Digital Culture". *Information Society* 22(2): 63–75.

Feher, K., D. Junaidy, D. Larasati, and A. Kovacs. (2017) "Creative Industries and Digital Economy – Perspectives from South East Asia and Central Europe." In T. Novak (Ed.), *Go Hungary – Go Indonesia: Understanding Economic and Business Issues* (151–172). Budapest: Budapest Business School, University of Applied Sciences. Search in Google Scholar

Gere, C. (2002). *Digital Culture*. London: Reaktion Books.

ICOM. (2020) Museums, Museum Professionals and Covid-19. https://icom.museum/wp-content/uploads/2021/07/Museums-and-Covid-19_third-ICOM-report.pdf

Kizhner, I., M. Terras, M. Rumyantsev, V. Khokhlova, E. Demeshkova, I. Rudov, and J. Afanasieva. (2020) "Digital Cultural Colonialism: Measuring Bias in Aggregated Digitized Content Held in Google Arts and Culture." *Digital Scholarship in the Humanities*. https://doi.org/10.1093/llc/fqaa055. Search in Google Scholar

Lischer-Katz, Z. (2020) "Archiving Experience: An Exploration of the Challenges of Preserving Virtual Reality." *Records Management Journal* 30(2): 253–274. https://doi.org/10.1108/RMJ-09-2019-0054

Minh, A. (2020) "Vietnam Approves $2.6 Billion Support Package for Covid-19 Crisis Victims." Vincetere. Available online at: https://e.vnexpress.net/news/business/economy/vietnam-approves-2-6-billion-support-package-for-covid-19-crisis-victims-4082541.html (accessed November 2, 2021).

NEMO. (2020) Survey on the impact of the COVID-19 situation on museums in Europe Final Report. https://www.ne-mo.org/fileadmin/Dateien/public/NEMO_documents/NEMO_COVID19_Report_12.05.2020.pdf

Peacock, D., and J. Brownbill. (2007 March) "Audiences, Visitors, Users: Reconceptualising Users of Museum on-line Content and Services." *Museums and the Web 2007*. https://www.museweb.wiki/resources-peacock-brownbill-audiences-visitors-users/

Sadiku, M. N. O., M. Tembely, S. M., Musa, and O. D. Momoh. (2017) "Digital Culture." *International Journals of Advanced Research in Computer Science and Software Engineering* 7(6): 33–34.

Sidel, M. (1997 September) "The Emergence of a Voluntary Sector and Philanthropy in Vietnam: Functions, Legal Regulation and Prospects for the Future." *Voluntas: International Journal of Voluntary and Nonprofit Organizations* 8(3): 283–302.

Soren, B. J. (2005) "Best Practices in Creating Quality Online Experiences for Museum Users." *Museum Management and Curatorship* 20(2): 131–148. https://doi.org/10.1080/09647770500402002

Thomas, S., and Mintz, A. (1998) *Virtual and the Real: Media in the Museum*. New York: American Association of Museums.

Uzelac, A. (2010). "Digital Culture as a Converging Paradigm for Technology and Culture: Challenges for the Culture Sector." *Digithum* 12: 25–31.

Vietnam News. (2020) Digital Transformation in Việt Nam: From Aspiration to Reality. https://vietnamnews.vn/economy/829504/digital-transformation-in-viet-nam-from-aspiration-to-reality.html

Vietnam News. (2021) Việt Nam Targets Further Digital Transformation in 2022. https://vietnamnews.vn/economy/1109594/viet-nam-targets-further-digital-transformation-in-2022.html

Vincetera. (2018) Cultural Trends in Vietnam: Five Experts Share their Insights. https://vietcetera.com/en/cultural-trends-in-vietnam-five-experts-share-their-insights

vom Lehn, Dirk, and Christian Heath. (2005) "Accounting for New Technology in Museum Exhibitions." *International Journal of Arts Management* 7(3): 11–21. *JSTOR*, http://www.jstor.org/stable/41064849 (accessed November 6, 2022).

Yilmaz, V., and H. Celic. (2011) "Extending the Technology Acceptance Model for Adoption of e-shopping by Consumers in Turkey." *Journal of Electronic Commerce Research* 12(2): 152–164.

1 Digital Culture and Digitization in Asia and the Global South

Introduction

This chapter provides an overview of digital transition and development of the cultural industries in Asia. It discusses national digitization strategies and projects in China, Japan, and South Korea as well as some examples from South East Asia in relation to national policy on digitization and the development of the creative industries. It also discusses the development of the creative industries in Europe and the USA to provide context on how government and private funding is essential for the development of the cultural industries. An example here shows how much support and funding was put into the creative industries across Europe during and after the Covid-19 pandemic. It is important here to provide a regional and global context in order to avoid cultural essentialism.

This chapter provides an overview of how work in the cultural sector is changing due to developments in digital technology. It discusses social media use and how it is now being harnessed for work. It will also state how social media platforms are conducive for cultural professionals' work due to being able to combine different types of media, being able to create new meanings with existing content, as well as being immediate, informal, and allowing a direct connection to the community.

This chapter introduces the concept of digital culture, specifically in relation to the digitization of art and use of new technologies and the ways that digitization is being applied to culture for preservation and content creation. With this, it will explore how developments in use of digital platforms have led to the formation of a more comprehensive digital culture, as opposed to only being 'signposts' for the physical space and not showing just digital copies of the physical. It will also consider the ethics of digitization in the Global South and what constitutes meaningful access.

The chapter discusses the issues of digital colonialism, whereby Western tech giants have the power to create regulations and policies that do not 'fit' with local values, ways of working, or communication style on Facebook in Vietnam. There are also biases in algorithms that overrepresent Western

DOI: 10.4324/9781003352792-2

culture and values while under- or mis-representing other cultures. This will be discussed in relation to the digital inequalities around inclusion and the pressure of having to use 'Western' or foreign technology (over national localized technologies), with reference to studies that explore how the use of social media is controlled by Western tech giants like Google and Facebook. However, this discussion will be positioned alongside the opposing argument of digital empowerment, whereby populations in the Global South can be empowered by being able to participate and have their voice included.

Digital Transition in the Culture Sector in Asia

Developments in digital transition in the cultural sector across Asia are being led by China, Japan, and South Korea. In these three countries, many large-scale, state-funded digitization projects are being carried out for the preservation of cultural heritage across Asia. China is investing large amounts of state funding and personnel into digitization projects; this is country-wide from central to local level for the digitization of cultural heritage at state institutions. For example, there are state-supported and state-led activities to digitize intangible cultural heritage in some of China's second-tier cities like Nanyang and Kaifeng (Zhou, Sun, and Huang 2019). Meanwhile, there have been developments in Japan to create a common archive and a standardized procedure for retrieval of archival data for the purposes of cultural preservation (Togiya 2013), specifically to preserve and share collective memories of national disasters. While a lot of digitization projects are taking place in Japan and South Korea, it is not happening on such a wide-ranging, country-wide scale as China.

Developments in digitization in the cultural industries in South East Asia, such as in Malaysia and Singapore, are taking place for the purposes of developing international connections and for developing national economies. In Malaysia, there has been a push by the government to connect both fields of digital technology and creativity, with the creative industries becoming a focus area for the Malaysian Government (Barker and Adrian 2017). In Malaysia, this is being developed effectively and systematically by the government, through putting standards and policies in place. In Malaysia, the government has begun to manage digital resources and has begun to create standard procedures that can adequately and effectively maintain and preserve digitized resources. The Malaysian government has identified areas that need to be addressed to ensure sustainable and successful implementation of digitization projects. Hence, developments are taking place on digital culture policy and using digitization for preserving cultural heritage in the cultural industries in East Asia as well as other parts of South East Asia.

The cultural sector in Vietnam includes editing (books, newspapers, magazines, sound recording, etc.), film, video, radio, and television activities, performing arts, press, museums, archives, libraries, wholesale and retail of cultural goods, and architectural activities. Vietnam has a diverse, rich, and unique culture represented by traditional culture (heritage, relics, festivals, traditional handicrafts, traditional arts) and contemporary cultural values (museums, contemporary art performance centres, new art forms), which have great potential for facilitating the development of cultural industries. In addition, thanks to the right policy of economic and cultural development, in the recent years, especially after the policy of socialization of cultural activities, different economic sectors have been involved for the development of various fields of cultural industries, such as film, music, fashion, performing arts, such as audiovisual firms, entertainment, craft production, fine arts, and craft villages (Ngo et al. 2019). The cultural industry combines three elements: innovation, the distribution of goods through modern infrastructure and production technology, and the ability to produce cultural products for economic benefit. In Vietnam, there are 12 cultural industry groups: advertising, architecture, software and entertainment, handicrafts, design, cinema, publishing, fashion, performing arts, fine art/photography/exhibitions, television and radio, and cultural tourism (Dan 2018). Consumption of cultural industry contributes to economic growth cannot be ignored and the culture's role in promoting the development of other industries is obvious. Therefore, to stimulate economic growth in Vietnam, there needs to be policies to promote the development of the cultural industry.

However, the contribution of culture to the economy has gradually been acknowledged. In 2020, Vietnam Government outlined a strategy for "national digital transformation by 2025" to create socioeconomic development and to allow the country to take an active role in the fourth industrial revolution (Vietnam Government 2020). This includes digital government, digital economy, and digital society. There is so far nothing specifically focused on digital culture. As Long (2021) states, "the national digital transformation program has a dual purpose of both developing digital government, digital economy, digital society and establishing Vietnamese digital businesses with global capacity". The Vietnam Government has prioritized nine sectors for digital transition: finance and banking, healthcare, education, agriculture, transport, logistics, energy, natural resources, and environment and manufacturing (Vietnam Government 2020). Some of the main objectives in digital transition in these sectors include: 80% of public services to go online with access via mobile devises, 50% of banking operations by customers to be fully online, fibre optic internet infrastructure to cover 80% of households, and 100% of districts (Vietnam Government 2020). As Samuel (2021) notes, Vietnam has made developments in the digital economy with, for example, the internet economy growing 16% from 2019 to US$14 billion, among the highest in South East Asia. Vietnam is projected to grow its digital economy from 2020 to 2025 by 29%, in second place across South East Asia behind the Philippines at 30%. However, Samuel (2021) also notes that while Vietnam has made important progress, more work needs to be done to address the digital skills development gap. In particular, a digital culture policy is necessary for effective, sustainable digital transformation and digitization practices in the cultural sector, and this is also important for the work of nonprofit art spaces and independent artists to receive support, common standards and procedures, and to ensure content is made accessible.

Developments in the cultural industries in Vietnam has also been due to developments in socio-economic status and foreign investment. The Vietnam Government's Sixth National Congress in 1986 set out the Doi Moi (Reform) direction to build a multi-sectoral commodity economy and open up investment cooperation with foreign countries. On that basis, the National Assembly introduced the Law on Foreign Investment in Vietnam in 1987. This was a turning point in the perception and views of the Party and the State on Foreign Direct Investment (FDI) – a precondition for opening the market and attracting FDI, regarded as a completely new and important resource for the country's socioeconomic development, and a positive contribution to the country's development. FDI has played a vital role in the push to provide vital resources for development. Ten years after "Doi Moi", as a result of the FDI, GDP annual growth rate in Vietnam reached 8.2%" (Ministry of Planning and Investment 2016, 4). However, changes have taken place in the strategic direction of FDI attraction due to changes in the global, regional, and domestic economic context (Ministry of Planning and Investment 2016, 6). The country no longer needed so much foreign investment as it developed to a low-middle income country. As a result, "the size of the global FDI inflows tends to decrease" (Ministry of Planning and Investment 2016, 6).

Vietnam has shifted from a centrally planned to a market economy has transformed the country from one of the poorest in the world into a lower middle-income country within one generation (World Bank 2022). This has been due to economic reforms since the launch of Đổi Mới in 1986, coupled with beneficial global trends. Between 2002 and 2021, GDP per capita increased 3.6 times, reaching almost US$3,700. Poverty rates (US$1.90/day) declined sharply from over 32% in 2011 to below 2% today (World Bank 2022). Vietnam was one of only a few countries to post GDP growth in 2020 when the pandemic hit. GDP growth slowed down to 2.58% in 2021 due to the emergence of the Delta variant but rebounded to 5.5% in 2022. Vietnam's development aspirations are to become a high-income country by 2045. To do this, the economy would have to grow at an annual average rate of around 5% per capita for the next 25 years. Vietnam also aims to grow in a greener, more inclusive way and has committed to carbon neutrality by 2050 (World Bank 2022).

There are inequalities in terms of budget and resources in the cultural sector globally. The state of the cultural industries is also about how much importance the government places on the cultural sector and the economic development stage of the country. As Mumtaz and Smith (2022) state, in relation to the developments of the cultural industries in Asia,

> the current level of development in a particular country, the specialized mix of products and services that it produces in its creative industry, its sensitivity to the performance of the creative industry across the global landscape, and its ability to generate improvements within its creative industry while minding the risk that it takes on will all be important considerations of the determinants of the creative economy in Asia.

For example, some European countries are far advanced in digitization, as well as other Asian nations such as China and Japan and South Korea. NEMO (2020) found that art and design museums across Europe have digitized an average of 65% of their collections. This is partly because there has been a long history of development in the creative industries in Europe, a lot of government funding and support, strong cultural policies, and an emphasis on making culture accessible online and usable for audiences. For instance, Benson and Stitzlien (2019) state that standardized rights statements and licenses for digital collections and institutional repositories across Europe have been available with Creative Commons licenses since 2001 and RightsStatements. org since 2015 and, in the USA, there are 12 distinct statements that can be used by cultural heritage institutions to communicate the copyright and re-use status of a digital object to the public (Benson and Stitzlien 2019), making it easier and safer to publish content online. While in Vietnam without proper, comprehensive copyright laws and enforcement, many cultural professionals are scared to publish their work. In addition, there is also stable internet connection and infrastructure, skills training, copyright protection, and access to high-quality digital equipment across Europe and the USA (Benson and Stitzlien 2019). Research and funding has also been accessible across Europe and in the USA to develop and recover the sector during and since the Covid-19 pandemic.

This discussion about national development of the cultural sector is important to consider because the use and application of a European definition of the cultural industries cannot necessarily be directly translated into an Asian context. A European definition is often adopted and applied in analyses of the cultural industries in Asia (Barker and Beng 2017; Roecker, Mocker, and Novales 2017). As Oyama (2019) argues, these models often "clash with the global cultural industries model". Lim and Lee (2018) argue that the simple uptake of the definition of cultural industries from Europe is problematic, as it is likely to assign one set of values from British, Anglophone, and European contexts that might not be applicable in many Asian contexts. For this reason, the nature and current transition of the cultural industries in some parts of Asia, especially in the Global South, have not truly informed the global conception of the cultural industries. As Lim and Lee (2018) point out, the development of the cultural industries in Asia is rarely included in discourse on the cultural industries in Europe and the USA. This book is part of the call and action to include Asia's role in the development of the cultural industries through digital transition.

Use of Digital Platforms and Social Media in the Arts

Globally, digital technologies today afford cultural professionals and artists with new ways of exhibiting art and culture online in digital environments. The digital environments of galleries and museums, including websites, apps, and social media platforms, have become curated spaces with the use of multi-media, interactive content and large amounts of digitized art collections. This links to Miles (2018, 21) who calls this "digital staging", as a result of more performances, curated experiences, and the sharing of processes and episodic narratives.

Moreover, content on digital platforms is no longer just a copy of the physical space. Digital artworks and virtual experiences are not a copy of the physical or original. Cultural professionals and artists now realize the potential of digital space and the specific affordances of digital platforms to produce new meaning with the content they share, they can create new meaning and new ways of showing things, like through process and journey and with a story because digital platforms allows for remediation. Digital platforms allow for the combination of different mediums and types of content, which means content can assume new meaning or can be applied to new contexts. The affordance of digital platforms is for recontextualization of content. This can be done on social media platforms as they allow for a combination of different mediums and types of content, remediation, and intertextuality. As Wodak and Reisigl (2009) argue, content can be recontextualized away from its prior context and, as Russo and Watkins (2005) argue, online cultural institutions act as continuously remediated environments, enabling audiences to make meaning in new ways.

In particular, the use of social media in the cultural sector has increased over the past few decades. This is due to the fact that social media affords both sides – the organization and audience – with specific things that websites, apps, etc., do not. As Pearlman (2015) argues, social media has become an invaluable tool to help artists, arts organizations, and audiences to connect, publicize, and exchange content. Social media sites provide cultural professionals with agency and to be able to publish professional content and connect with their community informally and live, but also to use informal content from their audience. Social media allows fast communication and the ability to receive direct response from the audience. As Hausmann and Poellmann (2013) argue, Facebook "allows for fast reactions, exchange of short messages and dialogue with target groups can happen quickly and easily". Mustika and Mahmudah (2021) argue Facebook "can make an impact quickly and thoroughly. The success via social media is because of its high penetration rate in the community". The developments in the use of social media have enabled better engagement, interaction, and dialogue with the audience.

However, there are controls and limitations with using these social media platforms. While cultural professionals operate with strong arts-centred beliefs and their work is about providing social good, there is a pressure to be more like a business on social media in order to attract sponsors, the audience, and to be more visible and create sharable/findable content on for-profit social media platforms. There has been an increasing use of social media in the arts amongst arts and cultural organizations for the purpose of marketing and conveying messages based on their need to attract sponsors to survive (Lee et al. 2014; Yue 2021). In particular, arts marketing on social media is becoming increasingly popular amongst nonprofit cultural institutions as a way to engage audiences (Stanoeva 2019; Wiid and Mora-Avila 2017). As Yue (2021) argues, "amidst the Covid-19 pandemic, nonprofits' available resources and budgets are stretched even thinner[...]and it becomes crucial for nonprofits to create virtual communication that is engaging and effective". The Covid-19 pandemic has accelerated developments in digitization practices and use of social media. It has also allowed many cultural practitioners to see the importance of making resources accessible online.

There are also time pressures and skills required in using Facebook for cultural professionals. professionals need to consistently and frequently post on Facebook, daily activity is essential, and they need to keep monitoring comments, responding to comments, and keep in contact with experts to show reputation and trust (Hausmann and Poellmann 2013). Cultural professionals are required to balance the content between text and image, which can be difficult in dual language. Cultural professionals must know how to open the posts to the share function and be knowledgeable about SEO and hashtags so content is easily searchable and shareable. More recently, there has also been more pressure to show 'behind the scenes' work and to make posts into digital storytelling.

Social media platforms can be conducive for building and supporting local community. This can be seen in grassroots movements by nonprofits for sharing care and creating community, especially since the Covid-19 pandemic. This type of communication has been highlighted in other parts of the South East Asia region during Covid. For instance, Mustika and Mahmudah (2021) note there has been the emergence of grassroots, nonprofit philanthropic movements on Facebook by nonprofit organizations to help society affected by Covid-19 in Indonesia. The nature of Facebook with its interpersonal communication and friendship links have helped these organizations to share their messages and to enable them to form local communities. Facebook can be used to facilitate 'neighborhoods', with "new forms of cooperation and community, created from the bottom up[...]that promote socialization" (Mosconi et al. 2017). As Briones et al. (2011) argue, the American Red Cross uses

Facebook to build relationships because "communication can be tailored to appropriate publics. Rather than only connecting distant people, Facebook is being used for people living in the same area". This also demonstrates how people can tailor Facebook to local cultural and timely needs. This will be explored in relation to cultural professionals' use of Facebook for building local community and sharing a culturally relevant and timely relevant rhetoric of care through art and events during the Covid-19 pandemic in Chapter 3.

Digital Content Creation and Digital Culture

Current priorities in the cultural sector are predominantly in digitization and digital content creation, with specific attention to the digital preservation of cultural heritage globally. In Asia, there is focus on the production of sustainable digital archives, where the quality of digital copies is of upmost importance for cultural preservation. With the increasing creation of digital art and experiences, there is emerging discourse/discussion on ethics of digitization in the Global South that explores the concerns around how to digitize artefacts and art collections ethically and appropriately amongst indigenous communities and for specific intangible cultural heritage in Asia (Ocón 2021; Pawelec et al. 2019). Ethics is necessary to discuss with the creation of digital culture because this can be an unequal process globally. As Punathambekar and Mohan (2019, 23) argue, "the profoundly unequal relations of power that share digital cultures and in particular the dominance that platforms like Facebook wield". We should also question the appropriateness of digitization for cultural preservation, in terms of whether it can provide accurate 'copies', enough information, and sufficient detail. In addition, the ethics of digitization in the Global South should also be about whether the highest-quality and most culturally appropriate technologies are available as well as sufficient staff and budget in order to produce high-quality, enough amount, and at a timely pace.

Developments in cultural professionals' use of social media for arts communication and publishing digital content are now leading to a shift – from creating digital content to creating digital culture. The importance of digitizing properly, therefore, is to create digital culture rather than just digital records or copies for storage. This is similar to Alsina (2010) who talks about the shift from the digitization of culture to digital culture, in terms of the impacts of digital technologies in the field of culture and how technologies are changing culture in terms of ways of living, feeling, and doing. Alsina (2010) states "the frontiers between the digitization of culture and digital culture are melting away".

However, what about the creation of digital culture and the factors that may affect the production of digital culture in the Global South? A lot of literature on digital culture comes instead from Western scholarship and from the media and communications field related to cyberculture and internet culture. This book fills a gap in discourse about digital culture by being about how culture is being digitized and digitally displayed, hence with more emphasis on the culture aspect of 'digital culture'. For example, scholarship explores the craze of selfies on social media as a cemented part of digital culture (Miller 2020) and the sheer extent of the presence of digital technology in our lives indicates the existence of a digital culture (Gere 2002). Digitization can be considered part of culture because it includes artefacts and systems of meaning and communication, which clearly demarcate contemporary lifestyles that are reflective of each historical moment and change over time. Digital culture today includes the practices, processes, and final product. Uzelac (2010) also makes clear that information and communication are also forms of culture, rather than only an exchange of messages. Hence, communication on social media – as with arts communication that includes artworks and text – can be a form of digital culture. Digital culture, in this sense, can be inclusive of audiences' participation as well as the content published on social media by cultural professionals.

The 'materials' used to display art today includes social media platforms. What is published on social media platforms is akin to a digital bricolage or a palimpsest of culture, with content being uploaded, adapted, and added to each day. As Deuze (2006) argues, digital culture comprises participation, remediation, and bricolage. Deuze (2006) understands remediation as the remixing of old and new media, which we see with artworks being digitized and displayed online. Deuze (2006) sees bricolage as the assembly, de-assembly and re-assembly of 'mediated reality'. This is about, for instance, how personal stories are being shared online. We all now become active agents in creating meaning or in creating content online. Cultural professionals, along with their audience, are active participants in sharing their version of contemporary Vietnamese culture – they update and modify stories through remediation and they assemble particular versions of culture. This leads to a new set of practices and changing the ways we give meaning to culture and our lives. This is what Deuze (2006) means by remediation, but what I call recontextualization in Chapter 3.

Today, we see the shift of culture to computer-mediated forms of production, distribution, and communication. Uzelac (2010) argues that digital technologies are challenging our understanding of culture. As it changes much quicker and is updated all the time on social media. Uzelac (2010) views digital culture as

> a new social system that determines experiences and opportunities for the citizens of today. Digital technologies and the networked environment have introduced new practices, opportunities and threats, and the culture sector needs to find appropriate ways for operating in this new reality.

Digital culture is the confluence of technology and culture. Technology is more than just code and numbers because it has its own essence and being. Social media, like other technology, is a tool or instrument for us to do something. By publishing on social media, we are revealing something about culture, and bringing forth something that was previously 'hidden' from large-scale, global view (taken from Heiddegger 1977). Alternatively, as McLuhan (1964) argues, the medium is the message – it is the medium that provides a way of being, of living, experiencing, and feeling. This is how culture is now being presented to audiences, and it is these digital technologies (specifically social media platforms) that are ordering and structuring our world today. We are seeing culture through the lens of technology. As Heidegger (1977) argues, technology is not neutral and this is why it is important to next discuss power dynamics globally in inclusion and access as well as an ethics of digitization.

Digital Empowerment vis-a-vis Digital Colonialism

Digitization includes two stages of initial digitization such as with scanning and creating metadata files, and, publishing this content onto digital platforms to make it accessible. This can be seen as two phases as well because digitization used to be more for the scanning and archiving. The first phase can be seen as 'digitization for cultural preservation' and the second as 'digitization for public access'. While the first stage provides cultural actors with the ability to preserve, archive, and store, the second stage affords them with many opportunities. For instance, it enables them to share Vietnamese resources with audiences and enable the audience to have greater access to more materials. In addition, the second stage enables cultural professionals to curate content and share stories as well as to communicate cultural values, symbols, and motifs that they see as important to their culture. Making access to digitized content is a vitally important stage of the digitization process. As Shiloba and Bot (2009) argue, access is one of the main objectives of digitization and the primary purpose of digitization is to improve access to digital resources.

This demonstrates how digitization can be a form of empowerment in the Global South. We can see how individuals can be empowered through the use of technology, from referring to what Mäkinen (2006, 390) says:

> With information technology people gain new abilities and ways to participate and express themselves in a networked society. This can be called digital empowerment, which is not a direct consequence of having and using technical facilities, but a multi-phased process to gain better networking, communication and co-operation opportunities, and to increase the competence of individuals and communities to act as influential participants in the information society.

This is a form of empowerment where people can use technologies as tools for *their own* purposes. As Mäkinen (2006) states, "empowerment is used in the sense of enablement, i.e., enabling people to do what is important to them, and enabling people to grow as competent subjects who have control over their lives and surroundings". Other theorists also argue that digital technologies can be a form of empowerment for communities in locations/regions outside the traditional 'centres' (Hjorth and Arnold 2013; Mignolo 2013). For instance, Mignolo (2013) looks at how an art institution in Qatar is challenging Western preconceptions of Muslim societies. This is what Mignolo (2013, n.p.) refers to as "cultural-ideological shifts" that are "part of a larger and complex deWesternising move, which points towards a multipolar world perspective that is emerging in the sphere of art and ideas". Mignolo (2013) also looks at the case of how museums in Singapore are now "institutionalising the memories of their own civilizations", which becomes "a symbolic act of cultural autonomy".

However, cultural professionals need to have enough available resources to be able to do this work effectively. For example, Pinto (2021) highlights a global disparity in resources, both capital resources (ownership and control of cables, servers and data) and intellectual resources (the most advanced technicians and research institutes); the other aspect is legal architecture, which blocks small countries from adopting policies that favour the production and purchase of goods/services produced domestically. So only perhaps with sufficient resources can they truly be empowered, in order to totally exploit and harness the potential of digital technologies, platforms, or social media for arts communication. "As we have seen the core principle of empowerment relies on achieving the full potential of an individual, community, and country, and in an information economy ICTs can be leveraged to achieve such an end" (UNESCO 2008). Hence, digital technologies can empower individuals and communities when there are no obstacles in digitization and making access. Ideally, digital technology can allow such communities to participate in global discourse and have control over their own representation. Dunn (2010) also hint to the issue of empowerment as being possible only if the conditions are alright, stating how developing nations could realize increased community empowerment especially where there are no critical impediments to access all forms of information and communication technologies.

However, this is arguably also visible now in digital space, as the 'centres' of culture and power create and circulate reps of 'others' and create the reps of other nation's art and culture. As Clayton (2009, 373) argues, there are "geographical processes of expropriation, in which people, wealth, resources and decision-making power are relocated from distant lands and people to a metropolitan center and elite". This is a form of digital cultural colonialism, which is the ability of Western online platforms to (over)represent the epistemologies of dominant communities while reforming the epistemologies of the world outside Western culture. This creates or results in the impression that places outside Western culture have less importance and acquire 'otherness' (Kizhner et al. 2020). As Morley and Robins (1995) argue, technology "reaffirms the essential supremacy of Western culture". This shows that, today, there is still an unequal access to and usage of the digital sphere. It is then the 'centres' that can create and define certain representations of 'others', as content online can represent these countries and cultures through certain stereotypes or through Western values.

Even with new technologies, Western discourse, stereotypes, and viewpoints of Asia still persist. More specifically, stereotypes and narratives on Vietnamese art and culture persist online. This results in imbalance and inequality in representation and in the amount of resources available online on art and culture and an imbalance in who/where gets to publish content. There is an imbalance in representation and inclusion related to content online, with a preference given to content created in the West and a higher amount of digitized art and cultural content from Europe and the USA, due to biases in algorithms. This is a form of "digital cultural colonialism", as Kizhner et al. (2020) argue, with "biases towards the West online" and "inherent biases in online cultural collections". A lot of cultural content online about Vietnam is framed with Western and orientalist epistemologies, with content online providing only limited representations. Such examples include images of tourist hotspots like Ha Long Bay, images of traditional clothes and customs, or images of war and conflict. The issue here has to do with power over access and representation on a global scale and who is in control of this representation and discourse about a culture. As Chaumont (2020) argues, preserving becomes the privilege of the hegemony; where technologically advanced countries get to define, choose, and provide cultural material for the rest of the world.[1]

Technology giants in the USA dominate the social media landscape in South East Asia and exert control in terms of access and usage. For instance, Google prioritizes data and sources from the West, with a large concentration of power and resources coming from the USA. For instance, digital platforms like Facebook are created and controlled by the West and shaped on Western ideology. This determines how it can be used by cultural professionals in Vietnam, as it uses algorithms and APIs that perpetuate existing biases, uses platform "terms and conditions" that reflect the morals and rights of Western societies, and includes technical requirements in translation from Vietnamese to English. From a postcolonial perspective, digitization processes in the Global South are a cause for concern as the dominance of foreign players and foreign ICT, and therefore foreign values perspectives, and ideas, resembles colonial structures (Pawelec et al. 2019).

This shows the important role these platforms occupy in capturing and reflecting our digital culture – can South East Asia content truly and meaningfully be included in this current context? As Bon et al. (2022) argue, despite the impact of digital technology on the lives and future of all people on the planet, many people, especially from the Global South, are not included in digital culture. This inequality is a systemic problem which we refer to this problem as "digital coloniality". We argue that to achieve a more equitable and inclusive global digital society, active involvement of stakeholders from poor regions of the world as co-researchers, co-creators, and co-designers of technology is required. A way to understand the impacts of digital transformation for people in the Global South is to observe the digital society through a decolonial lens. This helps to understand the, often tacit, patterns of power in the social and technological fabric. This led Bon et al. (2022) to carry out an exploratory design-science action-research project, dubbed Tibaŋsim, in Northern Ghana, to develop new modes of digital access and information sharing for rural communities.

The issue here is these platforms now exert control over developing countries even though they are at odds with local values. Another issue with this is that the use of social media can be different in parts of Asia, in comparison to the West, which can clash with some platform regulations and policies of tech giants in the USA. For example, Choi et al. (2011) points out the differences between South Koreans' use of social media sites, as less individualistic than in the West. As Flores-Fuentas and Navarro-Rangal (2020) argue, there is a conflict between Western apps and platforms that are designed for individual use and are relevant to Western values; however, they are used collectively in indigenous contexts. As Pinto (2021) argues, many countries are dependent on foreign technology that is Euro-centric value-laden and tailored for personal consumption instead of collective uses (referring to Facebook and Google). This demonstrates some of the cultural limitations of the technology and how professionals and users have to be adapt and tailor the platforms to other contexts. This will be discussed in terms of professionals' localization of Facebook and tailoring it to their own needs in Chapter 3. Local cultural values are embedded in communication on social media, hence, influencing communication style, type of content that is shared, and levels of connection with the audience/community and closeness in relationships between organization and audience on social media in Asia (Liu 2016; Yoon 2016;). For instance, Liu (2016) explores the concepts of trust, social capital, and reciprocity present in mobile communication in China, discussing how 'quanxi' – the values of relationships and social ties – influence the use of social media. Also, Yoon (2016) explores how local cultural norms are negotiated in South Koreans' media practices in relation to 'jeong' – the affective linkages between people – evident in visualizing feelings on social media (Yoon 2016). Others such as Hjorth and Arnold (2013, 30) have explored South Koreans' repurposing of Korean languages and traditions in new digital contexts and the locality of mobile media practices in Seoul.

Also, is it ethical and appropriate to have so much art and culture content on these Western-value-laden, for-profit, and friendship connection based platforms? Facebook makes visibility of nonprofits and independent artists' low and based on friendships. In relation to cultural archives and collections, as Acker and Kreisberg (2020, 6–8) argue, social media platforms govern access to cultural archives through the use of their APIs, platform policies, and terms of service – which "govern a set of possibilities for access" and how "the current access regime permits persistence problems for archivists who seek to provide access to collections". As it says on many posts now, you can choose 'most relevant', which means "Most relevant" is selected, so some comments may have been filtered out". But even if you select, 'all comments', it still says most relevant will be shown first'. As Banaji and Buckingham (2013, 15) argue, 'the Internet is a decentralized medium, and it is impossible to gain a comprehensive picture of everything that is available online, much less construct a representative sample of it'. Hogan (2018) argues that it is not possible to see everything that is posted on Facebook, which provides limitations in accessibility of content on Facebook. Furthermore, "social media sites use friendship connections to power key functionality for users, such as the organization of a newsfeed", meaning that users never see everything (Hogan 2018). As Hogan (2018) argues, APIs close off access to certain data and "work as technological gatekeepers" to data, posts, and info, as Facebook "sorts and filters these posts".

In this book, I wish to raise awareness of neglected issues and bring to light hidden challenges as well as acute practical challenges that cultural professionals have to face in the digitization process, but also just to highlight and neglected region of South East Asia. The nature of and current transition of the cultural industries in Asia has not truly informed the global conception of the cultural industries (Duester and Teague 2022). Moreover, the development of the cultural industries in Asia is rarely included in discourse on the cultural industries in Europe and the USA (Lim and Lee 2018). In a similar way, Heesen et al. (2019) strive to highlight neglected issues by exploring digitization in Africa and, in particular, the neglected issues of unequal power relations, neocolonialism, digital illiteracy, barriers to access, and the digital divide. Importantly, and as this book is evidence of, while literature talks about how outside companies and governments are putting in money, talent, and resources to digitize countries, it is really important for these people to digitize themselves, in the way they want to, with their own stories, homegrown. This shows that we must be aware of asymmetrical power relations and the need for developing countries to be able to use the technical resources provided in a culturally –relevant and – appropriate way. Majama and Quinn (2017) question the issues with foreign companies providing ICT infrastructure to African nations, in terms of how are digital technologies designed, and what impact this has on individual opportunities for action as well as societal futures. In the same way, Wakunuma and Masika (2017) explore the issues and ethics of cloud computing in Africa. While cloud computing has considerable potential for advancing development through the enhancement of capabilities, there remain huge challenges in its efficient, effective and ethical use. Wakunuma and Masika (2017) talk about the importance of ethics with foreign tech companies, as while there is a shared understanding of ethics across cultures, we should also recognize the need for some degrees of divergence across cultures. Bon et al. (2022) argue that despite the large impact of digital technology on the lives and future of all people on the planet, many people, especially from the Global South, are not included in the debates about the future of the digital society. This chapter has helped to fill this gap.

Summary

This chapter has provided an overview on the culture sector and digital transition in Asia. This has shown that most developments are being made (in terms of digital transition are taking place in China, South Korea and Japan (or at least this is what has been most documented/published). The places with the most comprehensive national policy on the cultural industry and those that have harnessed development in the creative industries – i.e. connecting culture to the economy – in South East Asia are Malaysia and Singapore. National policy is necessary for effective and sustainable digitization and an overall digital transformation and this is needed for nonprofits and independent artists. It has also been noted that there is not enough discussion of cultural industries development in Asia, as the West still influences discourse, so this book can be one of those resources to help redress the balance.

Developments in digital technology mean digital spaces now include curation, experience, digital storytelling, and direct communication with audiences. Digital platforms have now become environments that enable cultural professionals to curate and display visual content with specific tailored messages. Subsequently, these platforms are now dynamic and experiential 'living' spaces, being used for the display of art collections, sharing experiences, and holding events.

Art organizations and artists now know how to effectively engage the audience via social media. This can be for promotion, but discussion here has shown how promotion can be for social good. Furthermore, this has been emphasized during the Covid-19 pandemic with more art organizations using more caring language to appropriately engage the audience and to show the audience what solidarity means during a crisis. But there should be a consideration on how, what, to what quality content are being digitized and if this is ethical for developing countries in Global South. This is important to consider as it will impact the quality, pace, amount, what is selected for the publication online – and hence what kind of digital culture is created.

The discussion on this through this chapter also highlights how digitization and the creation of digital content is not always straightforward and simple, especially for those working in the Global South who face challenges in this process. Hence, the digitization process can be empowering for professionals but only to a certain extent due to these challenges, constraints, biases online, and existing/historic digital colonialism. Technologies and social media can be empowering, but only under certain conditions.

Overall, this chapter has highlighted the main gaps in the existing discourse (including literature, studies/reports, and research), showing the need for more discussion on: (1) making digitized content accessible and the notion of *meaningful* access for global south, (2) how digitization and display can empower cultural professionals and artists rather than only audiences, as is more commonly focused on, (3) the digitization of *contemporary* art/culture for cultural promotion rather than only preservation of heritage, (4) the struggles in digitization process, showing it is not always straightforward, (5) other actors from different parts of the world rather than just the West or powerhouses of Asia.

Note

1 The geopolitics of existing and emergent digital inequalities surrounding digitization and digital display can also be connected to literature on digital orientalism (Bahri 2019; Maitra and Chow 2015; Morley and Robins 1995). This explores how orientalist stereotypes still persist online today, which are created and circulated by the West and are extenuated by having to use Western digital platforms, technologies, and apps (Bahri 2019; Maitra and Chow 2015).

References

Acker, A., and A. Kreisberg (2020) "Social Media Data Archives in an API-Driven World." *Archives and Museum Informatics* 20 (1): 1–19. https://doi.org/10.1007/s10502-019-09325-9

Alsina, P. (2010) *From the Digitization of Culture to Digital Culture. Digithum: The Humanities in the Digital Era.* https://openaccess.uoc.edu/bitstream/10609/8799/1/n12-alsina-eng.pdf

Bahri, Y. (2019) "To where Is China running? Challenges and perceptions after 40 years of Chinese reforms, transformation, and integration into the world economy," Working Paper, No. 1908, Koç University-TÜSİAD Economic Research Forum (ERF), Istanbul.

Banaji, S. and D. Buckingham (2013) *The Civic Web: Young People, the Internet, and Civic Participation.* Massachusetts: Cambridge, MA: The MIT Press.

Barker, T., and Y. Adrian. (2017) "Making Creative Industries Policy: The Malaysian Case." *Kajian Malaysia* 35(2): 21–37. https://doi.org/10.21315/km2017.35.2.2

Barker, T., and L. Y. Beng. (2017) "Making Creative Industries Policy: The Malaysian Case." *Kajian Malaysia* 35(2): 21–37. https://doi.org/10.21315/km2017.35.2.2.

Benson, S.R. and H. Stitzlein (2019) Copyright and Digital Collections: A Data Driven Roadmap for Rights Statement Success. ACRL 2019 Proceedings. https://www.copyrightevidence.org/wiki/index.php/Benson_and_Stitzlein_(2019)

Bon, A., F. Dittoh, G. Lô, M. Pini, R. Bwana, C. WaiShiang, N. Kulathuramaiyer, and A. Baart. (2022) "Decolonizing Technology and Society: A Perspective from the Global South." In: H. Werthner, E. Prem, E.A. Lee, and C. Ghezzi (Eds.), *Perspectives on Digital Humanism.* Cham: Springer. https://doi.org/10.1007/978-3-030-86144-5_9

Briones, R., B. Kuch, L. Fisher, and Y. Jin. (2011) "Keeping up with the Digital Age: How the American Red Cross Uses Social Media to Build Relationships." *Public Relations Review* 27: 37–43.

British Council. (2013) "National Strategy for the Development of Cultural Industries in Vietnam to 2020, Vision to 2030." Available online at: https://www.britishcouncil.vn/sites/default/files/national-strategy-for-the-development-of-cultural-industries-to-2020-vision-2030.pdf (accessed April 28, 2021).

Chaumont, P. (2020) "Reshaping the Experiences in Art: Digitzation and 3D Archives." Available online at: http://digicult.it/news/reshaping-the-experience-of-art-digitization-and-3d-archives/ (accessed September5, 2020).

Choi, S., Y. Kim, and D. Sohn. (2011) "Cultural Difference in Motivations for Using Social Network Sites: A Comparative Study of American and Korean College Students." *Computers in Human Behavior* 27 (1): 365–372. https://doi.org/10.1016/j.chb.2010.08.015

Clayton, D. (2009) "Creative Innovation in the East Asia Arts and Culture Sector." Available online at: https://www.britishcouncil.org/research-policy-insight/insight-articles/creative-innovation-East-Asia-arts-culture (accessed January 26, 2021).

Duester, E., and M. Teague. (2022) "Redressing Digital Orientalism: How Vietnamese Cultural Professionals Are Harnessing New Digital Technologies To Reclaim the Narrative on Vietnamese Art And Culture." *Creative Industries Journal* 15(3): 272–292. https://doi.org/10.1080/17510694.2021.1938926

Deuze, M. (2006). "Participation, Remediation, Bricolage: Considering Principal Components of a Digital Culture." *Information Society* 22(2): 63–75.

Dunn, H. (2010) "Information Literacy and the Digital Divide: Challenging E-Exclusion in the Global South." In E. Ferro, Y. K. Dwivedi, J. Gil-Garcia, and M. D.Williams (Eds.), *Handbook of Research on Overcoming Digital Divides: Constructing an Equitable and Competitive Information Society* (pp. 326–344). Hershey, PA: IGI Global. https://doi.org/10.4018/978-1-60566-699-0.ch018

Flores-Fuentes, G., and Y. Navarro-Rangel. (2020) "Research Perspectives on Indigenous Knowledge and ICTs: A Decolonial Approach." *Educare* 24(2). https://doi.org/10.15359/ree.24-2.6.

Gere, C. (2002). *Digital Culture*. London: Reaktion Books.

Hausmann, A., and L. Poellmann. (2013) "Using Social Media for Arts Marketing: Analysis and Empirical Insights for Performing Arts Organizations." *International Review of Public and Nonprofit Marketing* 10(1): 143–161.

Heesen, J., K. Schopp, L. Schelenz, and M. Pawelec (2019) "Digitalization in the Global South." *TATuP Zeitschrift für Technikfolgenabschätzung in Theorie und Praxis* 28 (2): 10–51. https://doi.org/10.14512/tatup.28.2.s10

Heidegger, M. (1977) *The Question Concerning Technology and Other Essays*. New York and London: Garland Publishing.

Hjorth, L., and M. Arnold. (2013) *Mobile, Social and Locative Media in the Asia-Pacific*. New York: Routledge. Online@AsiaPacific. https://doi.org/10.4324/9780203584330.

Hogan, D. (2018) "The Presentation of Self in the Age of Social Media: Distinguishing Performances and Exhibitions." Online in *Bulletin of Science Technology & Society* 30(6): 377–386.

Kizhner, I., M. Terras, M. Rumyantsev, V. Khokhlova, E. Demeshkova, I. Rudov, and J. Afanasieva. (2020) "Digital Cultural Colonialism: Measuring Bias in Aggregated Digitized Content Held in Google Arts and Culture." *Digital Scholarship in the Humanities*. https://doi.org/10.1093/llc/fqaa055.

Lee, H.-R., H.-E. Lee, J. Choi, J. H., Kim, and H. L. Han. (2014) "Social Media Use, Body Image, and Psychological Well-being: A Cross-cultural Comparison of Korea and the United States." *Journal of Health Communication* 19(12): 1343–1358. https://doi.org/10.1080/10810730.2014.904022

Lim, L., and H.-K. Lee. (2018) "'Introduction' and 'Culture, Digitization, Diversity: Asian Perspectives.'" In *Routledge Handbook of Cultural and Creative Industries*. London and New York: Routledge.

Liu, J. (2016) "Credibility, Reliability, and Reciprocity: Mobile communication, guanxi, and protest mobilization in contemporary China." In S. Lim and C. Soriano (Eds.), *Asian Perspectives on Digital Culture: Emerging Phenomena, Enduring Concepts.* London: Routledge. https://doi.org/10.4324/9781315731650-6

Long, G. (2021) "National Digital Transformation Program to 2025, Orientation to 2030." ASEM Connect. http://asemconnectvietnam.gov.vn/default.aspx?ZID1=14&ID8=99391&ID1=2

Maitra, A., and R. Chow. (2015) "What's In? Disaggregating Asia through New Media Actants." In L. Hjorth,and O. Khoo (Eds.), *Routledge Handbook of New Media in Asia.* London and New York: Routledge.

Majama, N. S., and T. I. Magang 'Teddy.' (2017). "Strategic Planning in Small and Medium Enterprises (SMEs): A Case Study of Botswana SMEs." *Journal of Management and Strategy* 8 (1): 74–103. https://doi.org/10.5430/jms.v8n1p74

Mäkinen, M. (2006) "Digital Empowerment as a Process for Enhancing Citizens' Participation." *E-Learning and Digital Media*, 3 (3): 381–395. https://doi.org/10.2304/elea.2006.3.3.381

McLuhan, M. (1964) *Understanding Media: The Extensions of Man.* ISBN 81-14-67535-7.

Mignolo, W. (2013) "Enacting the Archives, Decentring the Muses: The Museum of Islamic Art in Doha and the Asian Civilizations Museum in Singapore." Ibraaz. https://aus01.safelinks.protection.outlook.com/?url=https%3A%2F%2Fwww.ibraaz.org%2Fessays%2F77&data=04%7C01%7Cemma.duester%40rmit.edu.vn%7C8abb0a1f8b314881dabe08d96da8ec85%7Cd1323671cdbe4417b4d4bdb24b51316b%7C0%7C0%7C637661394563188752%7CUnknown%7CTWFpbGZsb3d8eyJWIjoiMC4wLjAwMDAiLCJQIjoiV2luMzIiLCJBTiI6Ik1haWwiLCJXVCI6Mn0%3D%7C1000&sdata=46z%2B%2B92YeTTFrHTVx8NCMAuwpeRC%2FvEQl7CNkqg9VxY%3D&reserved=0 (accessed September 12, 2021).

Miles, I., and L. Green. (2008) "Hidden Innovation in the Creative Industries," NESTA report, July. Available online at: file:///C:/Users/v13008/AppData/Local/Packages/Microsoft.MicrosoftEdge_8wekyb3d8bbwe/TempState/Downloads/2008HiddenInnovationInCreativeIndustries%20(1).pdf (accessed January 6, 2021).

Miller, V. (2020) *Understanding Digital Culture.* London: Sage.

Ministry of Planning and Investment. (2016) 30 Years of FDI Mobilization in Vietnam: New Vision, New Opportunities in New Era. https://www.economica.vn/Content/files/PUBL%20%26%20REP/30%20Year%20of%20FDI%20in%20Vietnam.pdf

Morley, D., and K. Robins. (1995) *Spaces of Identity: Global Media, Electronic Landscapes and Cultural Boundaries.* London and New York: Routledge.

Mosconi, G., M. Korn, C. Reuter, P. Tolmie, M. Teli, and V. Pipek. (2017) "From Facebook to Neighbourhood: Infrastructuring of Hybrid Community Engagement." *Computer Supported Cooperative Work* 26(1): 959–1003. https://doi.org/10.1007/s10606-017-9291-z

Mumtaz, M. Z., and Smith, Z. (2022) "The Performance and Determinants of Creative Industries in Asia." In T. Sonobe, N. Buchoud, T. Tiong, S. Baek, N. Hendriyetty, and E. Sioson (Eds.), *CREATIVE ECONOMY 2030: Imagining and Delivering a Robust, Creative, Inclusive, and Sustainable Recovery* (pp. 84–102). Kasumigaseki: Asian Development Bank Institute (ADBI).

Mustika, R. and D. Mahmudah (2021) *Philanthropic Actions Via Facebook During Covid-19 Pandemic: A Study of Digital Ethnography. Proceedings of the 4th*

International Conference on Communication & Business (ICCB 2021). https://ssrn.com/abstract=3892653 or http://dx.doi.org/10.2139/ssrn.3892653

NEMO. (2020) Digitization and IPR at Museums in Europe. https://www.ne-mo.org/fileadmin/Dateien/public/Publications/NEMO_Final_Report_Digitisation_and_IPR_in_European_Museums_WG_07.2020.pdf

Ngo, T. L., T. V. H. Trana, M. D. Trana, Q. H. Nguyena, and V. H. Hoang. (2019) "A Study on Relationship between Cultural Industry and Economic Growth in Vietnam." *Management Science Letters* 9: 787–794. https://doi.org/10.5267/j.msl.2019.3.009.

Ocón, D. (2021) "Digitalising endangered cultural heritage in Southeast Asian cities: preserving or replacing?" *International Journal of Heritage Studies*, 27(10): 975–990. https://doi.org/ 10.1080/13527258.2021.1883711

Oyama, S. (2019) "In the Closet: Japanese Creative Industries and their reluctance to forge global and transnational linkages in ASEAN and East Asia." Accessible online: https://www.eria.org/publications/in-the-closet-japanese-creative-industries-and-their-reluctance-to-forge-global-and-transnational-linkages-in-asean-and-East-Asia/ (accessed June 12, 2021).

Pawelec, M., J. Heesen, L. Schelenz, and K. Schopp. (2019) "Digitization in the Global South, TATuP Zeitschrift für Technikfolgenabschätzung." *Theorie und Praxis* 28(2): 10–51, https://doi.org/10.14512/tatup.28.2.s10.

Pearlman, W. (2015) "Puzzles, Time, and Ethnographic Sensibilities: Research Methods after the Arab Spring." *Middle East Law and Governance* 7(1): 132–140. https://doi.org/10.1163/18763375-00701002

Pinto, R. A. (2021) "Digital Sovereignty or Digital Colonialism?" *SUR International Journal on Human Rights* 5(2): 15–27. https://sur.conectas.org/en/digital-sovereignty-or-digital-colonialism/

Punathambekar, A., and S. Mohan. (2019). Social Media Platforms. *BioScope: South Asian Screen Studies* 12(1–2): 170–173. https://doi.org/10.1177/09749276211026180

Roecker, J., M. Mocker, and A. Novales. (2017) "Digitized Products: Challenges and Practices from the Creative Industries." Conference Paper, AMCIS 2017 Strategic and Competitive Use of Information Technology (SCUIT).

Russo, A., and J. Watkins. (2005) "Digital Cultural Communication: enabling new media and co-creation in Asia." *International Journal of Education and Development using ICT* 1(4): 4–17.

Samuel, P. (2021) "Vietnam's Digital Transition Plan to 2025." Vietnam Briefing. https://www.vietnam-briefing.com/news/vietnams-digital-transformation-plan-through-2025.html/

Shiloba, G. E., and N. G. Bot. (2009) "Beyond Digitization: Access and Preservation." *Information Manager* 9(1). https://doi.org/10.4314/tim.v9i1.55476.

Stanoeva, I. (2019) "Social Media Possibilities for Improving Arts Marketing Performance." Proceedings of International Conference "Information and Communication Technologies in Business and Education". Publishing house "Science and Economics", University of Economics – Varna (pp. 247–256).

Togiya, N. (2013) "Trends in Digital Cultural Heritage in Japan, 1980–2012." *Art Libraries Journal* 38 (2): 11–16. https://doi.org/10.1017/S0307472200017971.

UNESCO. (2008) Reports prepared for UNESCO on the occasion of the International Association of Media and Communication Research (IAMCR) 50th Anniversary Conference 2007 Media, Communication, Information: Celebrating 50 Years of Theories and Practice (pp.78–102).

Uzelac, A. (2010). "Digital Culture as a Converging Paradigm for Technology and Culture: Challenges for the Culture Sector". *Digithum* 12: 25–31.

Vietnam Government. (2020) "2020 National Strategy for Digital Transformation to 2025, vision towards 2030." Available online at: http://vietnam.gov.vn/portal/page/portal/English/strategies/strategiesdetails?categoryId=30&articleId=10050825 (accessed April 28, 2021).

Wakunuma, K. and R. Masika. (2017) "Cloud Computing, Capabilities and Intercultural Ethics: Implications for Africa." *Telecommunications Policy*, 41 (7–8): 695–707. https://doi.org/10.1016/j.telpol.2017.07.006.

World Bank. (2022) The World Bank in Vietnam: Overview https://www.worldbank.org/en/country/vietnam/overview

Wiid, R., and Mora-Avila, P. (2017) "Arts Marketing Framework: The Arts Organization as a Hub for Participation." *Journal of Public Affairs* 18(2): 198–207. https://doi.org/10.1002/pa.1657

Wodak, R., and M. Reisigl (2009) "The Discourse-Historical Approach (DHA)." In R. Wodak and M. Meyer (Eds.), *Methods of Critical Discourse Analysis: Introducing Qualitative Methods* (pp. 87–121). London: Sage.

Yoon. (2016) "The Local Sociality and Emotion of Jeong in Koreans' Media Practices." In S. Lim and C. Soriano (Eds.), *Asian Perspectives on Digital Culture: Emerging Phenomena, Enduring Concepts.* London: Routledge. https://doi.org/10.4324/9781315731650-6

Yue, C. (2021) "Leadership Going Social: How U.S. Nonprofit Executives Engage Publics on Twitter." *Telematics and Informatics* 65(1): 101–137. https://doi.org/10.1016/j.tele.2021.101710

2 Digitization and Cultural Professionals in Vietnam

Introduction

Globally, an ever-increasing amount of cultural work is becoming digital. This has forced cultural professionals to work in more diverse ways, producing new types of content specifically for online platforms, finding new ways of communicating with audiences, and creating new meanings or applying stories to content. Digitization projects have been taking place in the cultural sector in Vietnam, including scanning images, objects, and photographs for preservation or to create digital archives. However, these digital archives and collections have – up until recently – not been publicly accessible but, rather, solely for preservation and archiving. Today, cultural professionals are starting to develop innovative ways of publishing and displaying digitized content by using new digital technologies and digital platforms. This is producing a paradigm shift in the nature of digital work practices for cultural professionals and a shift in the way of publishing and displaying culture. Digitization is no longer being used only for archiving and storage but also for promoting and providing access to culture. This reflects a change in practices amongst cultural professionals in Vietnam in terms of how they use digital technologies and the value they place on making cultural resources publicly accessible online. This can be seen as a shift from 'digitization for storage and archiving' to 'digitization for publishing, promotion and access'. As a result, this is creating an emergent digital culture, which is being created by Vietnamese about Vietnamese culture.

Cultural professionals are the pioneers in creating a digital culture. This chapter will show how cultural professionals are pioneering in creating accessible resources for use in education, cultural tourism, soft power for international relations, and for commercial purposes to boost the economy. As a result, it can be said that cultural tourism will be a spearhead of the cultural industry, in the coming time (Dan 2018). However, this can also be applied to contemporary arts and culture in Vietnam. This is an especially important moment in Vietnam because 'culture' and 'culture industry' are relatively new concepts and have only recently been acknowledged officially by the Vietnam Government. As Ngo et al. (2019) argue, even though the scale of the

DOI: 10.4324/9781003352792-3

cultural sector nearly doubled between 2012 and 2016, the cultural industries in Vietnam are still underdeveloped and less developed than other countries in the region. For instance, the economic and social value of the cultural sector has been harnessed in many countries, including China, Korea, and Japan. Relatively speaking, the cultural industries in Vietnam are at an early stage of development (Ngo et al. 2019). In 2013, culture was officially recognized as part of the economy and as the "cultural industries" in Resolution 33/NQ-TW of the 11th Party Congress (Ly, 2016). As Dan (2018) comments, the 'Cultural industry' is a new term for the economy and culture of Vietnam, only coming into use over the last three to five years. Since 2016, the term gained greater recognition when the Prime Minister approved Decision No. 1755/QD-TTg in 2016, outlining a strategy of developing the cultural industries until 2020 with a vision to 2030. The development of the cultural industries plays an important role in exploiting the economic potential of culture, promoting national identity, creativity, and innovation while empowering the nation in the age of globalization, digitization, and increased competition, as well as taking advantage of cultural resources in building the economy and international relations. This has been supported with international organizations and councils that have helped to position the cultural industries in Vietnam as key pillars of economic growth, such as the British Council and UNESCO.

Other Vietnamese cultural commentators who speak about current transitions in the cultural sector include designers and contemporary artists. As Tuan Le (2018, cited in Vietcetera) says, Vietnam is now about design and creativity – about innovating and producing content and products. These products, services, and content include aspects of our culture and country at their heart. "With design in Vietnam, there's been a long overdue incorporation of local identity", as Tuan Le says. He says many in Vietnam are now trying to break away and provide more diversity than only images of references to hems or straw hats. They want to redefine the contemporary image of Vietnamese culture. This showcases contemporary culture, rather than only cultural heritage, in terms of its impact on showcasing Vietnamese culture to the world and for national economic and cultural development. Comments by Richard Streitmatter-Tran (cited in Vietcetera 2018) also show how this is happening with specific regard to contemporary art scene in Vietnam. He comments that 2017 saw many Vietnam-based artists exhibit in major exhibitions both abroad and locally. For instance, international interest in Vietnamese art has been piqued by artists like Tran Trong Vu with "The Sonnet In Blue", an "extravagant maze of handmade flowers", at the National Gallery Singapore. And Vietnamese-born Mexico City-based artist Danh Vo had significant shows both in 2017 and already in 2018 – last year, he completed his Ng Teng Fong Roof Garden Commission for the National Gallery, Singapore, and this year his show "Take My Breath Away" was held at the Guggenheim Museum, New York. And there's also Dinh Q. Le's "Skin On Skin" at the 10 Chancery Lane Gallery, Hong Kong which opened in March – a show that includes a "series of woven photographs" that explore the evolution of attitudes towards sex in Vietnam.

Vietnam News (December 17th 2020) says 2020 was the starting year for the national digital transformation. It was also this year that saw a shift from simply digitizing documents and processes, as the development of digital technology allowed Vietnamese people, professionals, businesses to bring all of their operations, communications and products into cyberspace. Vietnam News comments on the three main areas of digital development, being "digital government, digital economy and digital society". However, they also recognize that there are issues and that Vietnam must keep up with other countries in this digital transition, saying that "in order to realise the aspirations for national development, Việt Nam must quickly seize the opportunity and implement digital transformation faster, stronger and more broadly". More needs to be done and more must keep on being done, as this is a long process. 2022 saw further digital transformation. In 2022, new strategies on digital infrastructure, data, technology industry, and technology enterprise in Vietnam were first implemented (Vietnam News, December 24 2021). In fact, the challenges of the pandemic have contributed to this fact as it has promoted the digital transformation process. As Vietnam News (December 24 2021) comments, in just a short time, the national digital transformation has spread widely at a rapid pace, creating a wave of digital transformation across ministries, branches, localities, agencies, and businesses across the country. In this digital transformation process, Vietnamese digital technology enterprises have demonstrated their pioneering role in research, development and innovation, mastering technology, and making important contributions to the development process of the digital economy. And in the cultural sector, cultural professionals have taken a pioneering role in development and mastering technologies to keep up with global digital transformation and the sudden shift to online during the pandemic.

Developments in Digitization Practices

Cultural professionals have been digitizing their artwork and art practices for the past three decades. However, some say they have been archiving their artworks for many more years. For instance, Participant 18 from Linh Duy says "I myself as a painter, and the galleries who work with me frequently, digitize artwork for archiving purpose. We have been doing this for a few decades, even when digital technologies were still new in Vietnam". A more widespread and commonplace acceptance of the importance of digitization for archival purposes started more recently. For example, artist Ngo Van San says digitization practices started to change within the last seven to ten years:

> I have had camera equipment since long time but only recently do I pay close attention to digitization. Before, about 10 years ago, I did not care much about keeping records of my paintings as digital files. I only took

photos of a few paintings which I am particularly happy with. I was lazy partly because it is effort-consuming and complicated to set up all the lighting system for a photoshoot. Now I am very attentive and I digitize almost all my artworks.

Today, cultural professionals digitize in myriad ways and more systematically. Moreover, this aspect of their practice is no longer solely for archiving. Participant 14 from Hai Dung says

we mainly take pictures and store them on Google Drive or Dropbox. We sometimes have videos. For video art, we will film. Every month Hai Dung has at lEast one exhibition and several concerts, which will be recorded. Now we also use livestream to reach those geographically faraway. We have a YouTube account but it is only for video storing rather than for promoting. We post pictures on Facebook, Instagram and our website.

As Participant 18 from Linh Duy says

Materials I upload are usually pictures of my artwork. Included also are narrative information related to artworks like: ideas, material, size, year of production. Besides, there are also pictures of exhibitions, media articles, interviews, other exchange activities, listed as 'news' items.

Participant 19 from Hai Duong says that since the past three years, "all activities are in digital mode and communicated online. Artworks are digitized at a faster speed. We invest more financial & human resources into this work".

For Participant 15 from Thuy Khoi, "digitization was something ad hoc, as and when we had time, staff, money, because we wanted to focus first on our own artistic practices. But the pandemic forced us to see importance of digital display".

This shows how digitization practices have changed and how digitization has now become a central aspect of their work practices. This reflects the general shift in the cultural sector globally towards more use of digital technology and digital platforms, tools, and apps in working practices. Participant 8 from Thao says "generally, digitization is becoming easier and more popular". Even though transitioning so much to digital, cultural professionals also highlight the common global concerns around the longevity and sustainability of digital technology. While there is a general shift to digital transition in the cultural sector in Vietnam, some are worried about relying too much on technology. Many are concerned with having to keep up with new technologies and updates of social media platforms. Others also worry that these platforms will become obsolete, like Participant 25 from Cat Ba who says

Even with the website, I am worried if it might get out of order or no longer exist. I want to use other methods (like using multiple spare portable hard drives or second website, etc.) but I cannot for now due to budget constraints.

Participant 16 from Cam Thuy also has concerns around the issue of technology going wrong or files being corrupted:

> If I do have (photos & videos), I will keep them in a hard drive. Facebook is not for archiving and the quality (of photos & videos) there is not high. Some people upload their videos for example to Youtube. Later as the videos they keep in their hard drive are lost, they have to reuse those in Youtube with a low quality. There is always that risk.

The purpose of digitizing has also changed recently. It is now for the purpose of publishing content onto digital platforms and for providing public access. The purpose of digitizing art and culture is now to allow the audience to view, experience, and interact. For example, AR and 3D technologies have been widely adopted over the last two years as a solution to online exhibition for a variety of art styles, such as photography, visual art, and performance art. As Participant 25 from Cat Ba says, "Some artists now publish their artworks on websites and some exhibitions and events are uploaded to website in 3D mode".

Today, there is also more diversity in *how* cultural professionals are publishing content. They are using a combination of new techniques, methods, and approaches. For example, digitization projects now include videoing and livestreaming. Also, artists' artworks or art spaces' art projects are more intertwined with digital technology including the use of 3D, VR, AR, and animation.

What they are digitizing is also expanding. More art styles are becoming digital, such as installation art and performance art. As Participant 11 from Hian says, "we will do more experimenting with ideas, like how to migrate experiential art to online. So we will continue with making more styles of art digital". In addition, some artists are also digitizing their working practices. As Participant 26 from Bien Hoa says

> I film my creative process or tell a story using videos which I will then upload to my Youtube channel. I have managed to build an audience base who are interested in viewing those videos. I will film the artworks which I feel happy with.

The artist posts videos of their working process on YouTube as a way to create a closer connection with the audience. This shift in digitization practices also reflects a shift globally in the art world towards documenting, *and now publishing*, the working process.

The discussion above highlights how artists but also art spaces are digitizing both the final product and the process. They do this in order to give the audience a more comprehensive view and understanding of their art. More importantly, this leads to the audience gaining a better understanding of Vietnamese culture. For instance, different digital tools and mediums are used to provide more information about their artwork and providing more 'angles' on their work. This provides the audience with better access to their work. This is common across many cultural professionals' work. For instance, Participant 24 from Ninh Binh says "I do take pictures of my paintings and record videos of my working process [...] show my creative journey". As Participant 25 from Cat Ba says, sharing her "working process as well as results is a directly visual method to help my audience to see and understand more clearly my work". Some even say that documenting the process becomes more important than only displaying the final product online: As Participant 17 from Hue Ho says "digitization helps with problem of process, especially today, as many artists no longer consider the final product as the most important thing but the process". This is felt across the world globally, where audiences and artists demand to see/show their process. Digitization of the process is understood today to help artists see their own process and function as a form of reflection. As Participant 18 from Linh Duy says "Today, digital technologies are no longer solely for the purpose of archiving; they become themselves mediums to convey ideas, channels of interaction; they are part of creative work and display processes". Digitization is now more accepted as an art form in itself – in the same way as a canvas or a camera.

The Motives of Digitization for Display and Access to Cultural Content/Resources

Providing a Diverse and Contemporary Image of Vietnamese Culture

One motive for digitizing with the aim of publishing it online is to provide the audience with content that reflects *contemporary* Vietnamese culture. This is so that both local Vietnamese audience realizes art can be contemporary, rather than only traditional – and – for updating international audiences' perspectives about Vietnamese culture. This means that, as Participant 22 from Bui Ne says, "It is even more important to share contemporary arts, which will help reflect the true image of modern life in Vietnamese society beyond outdated narratives".

There are also some who say it is vital to share a *contemporary* story or narrative with the content they share. For instance, Participant 13 from Ben Hai wants to convey contemporary life and culture in Hanoi to both local and international audiences, saying "what we want to provide and create is a digital record or diary of contemporary Hanoi". As Participant 27 from Tay Ninh says

> It is also a story of how Vietnam is no longer a country of war but of economic development, a story of creativity, of innovation, of contemporariness. It is neither a story about only traditional values nor a story about development or modernity. So via digital platforms, I imagine I am contributing to a big picture of Vietnam where development exists along deep-rooted traditions and cultural values.

They also want to increase the *diversity* of representation on Vietnamese art, in response to the limited and stereotypical image of Vietnamese culture online. For instance, the current Google search of 'Vietnamese culture' shows images of women wearing traditional clothing like the nón lá hat and ao dia as well as beautiful mountain views. As Participant 4 from Luc Nam says, "with the content we display online, we want to show the rich variety of styles and artists that shows the enormous diversity of the arts in Vietnam". They want to convey a message about the "diversity" in Vietnamese art, by showcasing the range and variety of Vietnamese contemporary art. Participant 8 from Thao also says "the message with what we have uploaded is about the diversity in works, genres and styles of Vietnamese art today".

As Tinh Dau studio says,

> I have talked to many foreign collectors and they told me that their experiences are now much better. They can under better the art and culture sector in Hanoi. Newly available content online really helped foreigners discover unseen and newer aspects of Vietnam and of young Vietnamese creative professionals. They are contributing to bringing about a change in Vietnam's image.

However, they do not want to challenge or resist stereotypes already existing online. Instead, they are pleased that digital platforms provide them with the opportunity to increase the amount of and range of representations online. What they share and what they do now is not to erase something already online. It does not correct or redress something. It is more about what they share. Participant 20 from Long Cai also suggests it is not their responsibility to change stereotypes but, instead, to utilize the opportunities of digital technologies to publish their own stories and narratives.

> The best way to replace the wrongful stereotypes is not to build other stereotypes. It is to democratize the representations. So that everyone can join and disseminate [his/ her own representation]. So instead of developing a digital collection of a single museum, we should instead give people freedom to represent themselves.

It is important for them to now be able to create their own stories about contemporary Vietnamese culture through the use of digital technologies to digitize and display Vietnamese art.

Addressing the Lack of Resources Online

Another motive of digitization for display and providing access to cultural content is to create more available resources online for education, research, and local/international audiences. Participant 20 from Long Cai says there is lack of resources online for educators. Participant 20 from Long Cai says about the global disparities in amount of content online and about redressing the imbalance in who dictates the narrative online about art and culture, and the opportunity of digital technologies for equalizing the 'playground':

> I am a lecturer [and an artist] and I need a lot of materials. As I teach courses about artwork statement or art history, I could not find the materials I need. I can only verbally describe those artworks to my students, that is ridiculous. However, digital platforms and digitization allows more voices to enter the discourse[…]Vietnam faces a lot more disadvantages compared to other countries[…]For example To Ngoc Van cannot 'compete' with Picasso. Of course we cannot say who wins over who if we compare their paintings. But Picasso is more widely appreciated than To Ngoc Van. Social network helps flatten the playground. If I post something on Instagram, my artworks have the equal position with those of someone from New York or Brooklyn. Such an equal playground is beneficial for Vietnam. If we are aware of that, we have to move forward and try to grab as much of that playground as possible before others win over us.

Making access to more Vietnamese resources can help redress the imbalance globally on the amount of resources that are available online about art and culture. Some respondents expressed their mission as working to increase the amount of available resources for education (young generation), researchers (locally and abroad), and the general public to redress the 'East/West' imbalance. They want to educate their audiences about art, make art more open/accessible to everyone, and show how art can be contemporary. Participant 7 from Thai Binh says there is

> too much content from the West online for resources and not enough on Vietnamese art and culture[…]We want to have more resources available for students here about Vietnamese art and culture as more resources used come from the West[…] we want to teach more about Vietnamese art and culture and show Vietnamese artists are just as important as Picasso.

Having more available resources online about Vietnamese art and culture as well as being created by Vietnamese cultural professionals will empower students, educators and the general public in Vietnam to see their culture alongside other cultures online, hence, valuing their culture more.

Participant 25 from Cat Ba says there is not many materials online, which impedes audience's access in terms of ability to understand Vietnamese art scene. Hence, this prevents people from 'true' access to and ability to learn about and understand Vietnamese culture properly.

> especially Vietnamese art, I find it difficult to find information. Artworks and practices of older generations of artists can only be known via some books, small pictures and thus are difficult to get a hold of. This poses serious limitations on the audience's senses, especially young audience who want to learn about and review practices of previous ages…I think public online sharing by today's young artists will be very useful for the audience and those who want to learn about art – those who are living far and cannot attend exhibitions or events. This will make the Vietnam art scene more diverse, colourful and clearer.
>
> (Participant 25 from Cat Ba)

An important aspect of addressing the issue with lack of resources online is that cultural professionals can increase the amount of resources *made by* Vietnamese cultural professionals. Reflections on this issue include the artist, Participant 25 from Cat Ba, who says,

> More sharing by Vietnamese artists on their practices via the world's common platforms will help foreign friends get a better hold of Vietnamese artists' developments, current interests, aesthetic views. It will enable more collaboration or help foreigners have a clearer, closer, more direct view rather than via intermediaries or a view already filtered by the media.

This shows how they feel there needs to be a self-created image of Vietnamese culture. As Participant 27 from Tay Ninh says, it is important *for them* to be able to create the image of Vietnamese culture because "If you are an outsider [geographically located outside Vietnam], it is difficult to produce a truthful documentation".

It is not done now so much by only others, as was the case in the past. However, such incomplete or singular/outside-perspectives and materials still exist online. Plus, there are still Western dominances. Participant 20 from Long Cai describes this in relation to Vietnamese art over the past 40 years:

> It is so frustrating that we could not study what other artists did before. People did amazing things but those artworks are not documented. We can

only rely on archives collected by Westerners but they only kept records of what they found interesting.

Moreover, even though they can publish and share content, they are forced to use foreign tech, agencies, funding bodies, with Western values and terms. Participant 20 from Long Cai says that, as an independent artist from Vietnam,

> we don't have the freedom to communicate democratically our own image. We are always dependent on a foreign agency. For example, 10 or 20 years ago, foreign funds only showed artworks about political topics. That is their orientation, maybe their audience loved to see those artworks. What they represent – or do not represent – is part of pre-defined agenda[...]As long as we are still dependent on any institutions to represent Vietnam, we are forever stuck in stereotypes, no matter what stereotypes.

Foreign agencies, councils, and funding bodies in Vietnam and outside have particular agendas and directions, to which these artists and culture professionals have to adjust their projects.

This is in contrast to earlier response about digital technology as more democratic and equalizing, with some cultural professionals who talk about the general opportunities of the internet for freedom and democracy. This gives them hope for more equal inclusion. Participant 20 from Long Cai says "digital technologies help flatten the playground. Such a more equal playground is beneficial for Vietnam...give ppl freedom to represent themselves". Multiple voices are needed to create digital resources, rather than just one museum for instance.

Tackling the Issues of Creating Meaningful Access

Providing access to art and culture content is now an essential part of and a key motive for doing digitization. However, there is also the feeling amongst cultural professionals that making something accessible is not so simple as uploading an artwork. Digitization needs to be done properly to be sustainable and meaningful (meaningful to them, their culture, and the audience) and to ensure there is "effective digitization" as Participant 6 from Ky Cung says, with a strategy for publication and communication with audience.

However, the 'second stage' of digitization is not an easy part of digitization, as it requires a lot of human, technical, and financial resources. It is something that needs to be acknowledged as important by government and put into policy. These cultural professionals see the importance of this aspect of digitization but how it needs to be promoted more and supported more at the national level. Yet, Vietnamese cultural professionals' ability to digitize sufficiently in comparison to other countries is visibly different, due to a lack of human, technical, and financial resources but also because the Vietnamese

Government are only just realizing the importance of access to culture for developing soft power assets, tourism, and the economy. As Participant 22 from Lang Son says, access should be an essential part of the digitization process:

> access is one essential part of and one main reason for digitization. Digitization can no longer be just for archiving[...]Lang San are keeping videotapes of old movies. Today they keep restoring and maintaining old damaged videotapes. At the same time, they are converting those movies to digital format, into HD or 2K resolution, of good quality. However, the limitation is that our tasks are only to restore and to convert movies digitally. We fail to bring the movies to the audience[...]For now, only people who are willing to pay can get access to our archive. Otherwise, it is difficult to access. In other countries, they are good at that aspect. There are 2 tasks, one of archiving and maintaining classic movies and one of bringing those movies to the audience. If you only archive to protect the cultural heritage while withholding it from the audience, it no longer counts as the heritage.

As Participant 9 from Lieu Giay says

> artistic self-awareness and conceptualization have to be particularly clear so that impacts created by the artworks on digital platform can be maximized. Otherwise, it will be just so-so as when we see a picture or a video of an artwork.

It also needs careful consideration so that it is engaging for the audience, like with inclusion of metadata, so that we ensure people can access the object and information properly and have a comprehensive understanding afterwards and use of smartphone platforms and tech so people can access. Participant 9 from Lieu Giay says "artworks on digital platforms must be provided with detailed information and guidelines for their experiencing. Otherwise, artworks remain inaccessible to the audience".

In a more abstract sense, cultural professionals make clear that access should not just be a one-way flow. They wish for audiences abroad to be able to access Vietnamese culture that they publish; simultaneously, they wish to be able to showcase and share the content they create. A recurring word in their responses is about creating meaningful access to Vietnamese art and culture is that it must include 'mutual access'. This refers to the importance of, first, giving global audiences access to Vietnamese art and, second, providing Vietnamese cultural professionals with access to the global discourse. For instance, Participant 5 from Bac Giang refers to these two flows or two ways of 'access' and how digital platforms allow this: "it allows us to publish and widely disseminate news and images of Vietnamese art to the world" and Participant 5 from Bac Giang also say that "people globally can find out about art, events, and information about Vietnam". Similarly, Participant 8 from Thao says how "digital platforms allow people from abroad to access Vietnamese art". Participant 7 from Thai Binh says "the opportunity of digitization is that we can use art as soft power to showcase Vietnam to the world. Artworks can act as national cultural assets". In this way, access signifies the ability to have a voice, position, and link to the rest of the world, to be able to produce content and be a part of the discourse.

Challenges in Digitization and Impacts on Digital Transition

There are three main practical/tangible challenges in their digitization practices and process. The three main challenges are: (1) lack of human resources, (2) lack of financial resources, and (3) lack of technical resources. This lack of resources and difference to other parts of the world is acutely felt by cultural professionals in Vietnam as a middle-income developing country. This relates to what Pinto (2018) says about a global disparity in resources, including capital resources (ownership and control of cables, servers, and data) and intellectual resources (the most advanced technicians and research institutes). The other aspect is legal architecture, which blocks small countries from adopting policies that favour the production and purchase of goods and services produced domestically. These challenges are hindering their adoption of digital technology, access to high quality technical equipment, and the pace of developments in digitization the quality of content they can produce. For instance, Participant 10 from Song Hong says that "digitization is a big job, there is lack of funding and lack of resources". Also, Participant 4 from Luc Nam says "there are difficulties is getting the best technical equipment for scanning". Participant 1 from Phò Dày says "challenges include the need for infrastructure for digitization, it's a high tech field that needs skill and budget". Participant 1 from Phò Dày mentions that "a lot of resources" are required for digitization; "there are challenges because we need budget and human resources" (Participant 1 from Phò Dày). Participant 7 from Thai Binh says there is a notable "challenge with human resources".

Due to lack of human resources, the first main challenge, there is a sense that many practices or parts of their practice have to be done by themselves, in what can be seen as a DIY culture of practice. For example, Participant 29 from Di An talks about lack of human and technical resources and how they have to do many jobs themselves:

Indeed in Vietnam, tools available for people engaged in digitization are very few. Even in our gallery, we have to make it in house and invest [in digitization] as we cannot outsource. [...]For that to work, we have to train our staff which is time-consuming also.

As Participant 19 from Hai Duong says "we do not own a professional team for this aspect so things are still limited". As sensed from previous paragraph, they feel the need for better support, infrastructure, standards, and policies. Participant 14 from Hai Dung also says how they did most of jobs themselves for the Into Thin Air project:

> we wanted to make it 100% virtual, so we went to learn how to do that. At that time, the AR tech emerged. We decided to make an app. We met an IT company and hired them to do so. We did not know how to digitize artworks and put them on the app, especially for installation works. At that time, the technology was not yet well-developed as now. Still, we had to do it. We did it all by ourselves. [...]It took us 2 years until 2018 to finish. [...]It costs a lot. [...]Time is another thing, it took a lot of time. [...]It took two years but that was also because we were busy with other projects, this was not full time, and sometimes we were tired so we just keep it for a while and then come back to it. If we have a proper and more human resource, with people only working on that, then it would be better. Because at that time it was only me working on that. And the team just supporting but not that much. And I had to connect the artists with the IT team all the time. And make sure that everything was ok, and the whole content of the app have to be written and I have to decide the font, colour and everything, design and everything.[...]we were overloaded. So, we wondered what about using virtual spaces to save efforts.

The second main challenge is lack of financial resources. Artist Participant 25 from Cat Ba stresses how expensive the digitization process is and how it is impossible without support from funding bodies: "To digitize artworks, for example to create a 3D online exhibition, is costly and highly technical so it counts as a big challenge for which support from different parties is required". Another challenge for independent artists is the cost of platforms; artist Participant 16 from Cam Thuy says paying for platforms is expensive: "it is very expensive to access those platforms [*ArtStation, DeviantArt, Vimeo*]. It is like a business in which they sell online space, 'digital land', to you". This also comes back to the discussion on access – they find it difficult to access the best quality tech equipment and platforms because lack of financial resources.

They face many financial challenges because they are independent or non-profit art organizations. This is because what they do is often not for profit. As a result, they rely on funding from international embassies/councils. They must apply for grants in order to fund projects. However, foreign investment (FDI) increased after the Doi Moi in 1986 and then, after ten years, FDI gradually decreased (Ministry of Planning and Investment 2016). After only ten years of "Doi Moi", as a result of the FDI, GDP annual growth rate in Vietnam reached 8.2%" (Ministry of Planning and Investment 2016, 4). "The size of the global FDI inflows tends to decrease" (Ministry of Planning and

Investment 2016, 6). This means there are now fewer funding opportunities. Due to this, they have had to find other sources of funding and collaborate internationally on projects. There is an issue here of having to tailor work towards what foreign funders want. As Participant 15 from Thuy Khoi says:

> we need money to create artworks. Of course there are artworks which do not require any fund. But there are other which need funding, they can even be very expensive. Then where does that funding come from? What are the missions of funders? What do they focus on? For example, British Council[1] recently focuses on creative spaces and heritage. The cultural funds will focus on certain topics. Some artists will apply for those funds. They are already interested in those topics and will seek to use those funds for their work. There is no governmental support for contemporary arts in Vietnam so we are dependent on foreign funds. For example, British Council requires their grantees to report on the outreach of the project.

The third main challenge is lack of technical resources. Participant 14 from Hai Dung talks about all the challenges of creating 100% virtual art project: "The challenge was technology, we were low tech and even the IT company had never done this before. Tech companies in Vietnam are not advanced. So trying to make high-quality artwork virtually is a really big challenge". This shows how the lack of technical advancements and skills and equipment availabilities in other sectors also have an impact on the cultural sector. Also, the GPS technology is not as advanced and as accurate as in other countries, which impacted the quality of Participant 14 from Hai Dung VR project 'Into Thin Air':

> the GPS in Vietnam is not that accurate, it's always about 30 meter difference, so different in comparison to other country like Japan, where it is one meter difference, so we have to think about the solution for that for example. So it took time for us to fit it [the virtual artworks] to the space.

Interconnected to the technical challenges is issues with security, because they are small orgs or individuals with little power or ability to control such threats. They don't have the necessary human, technical, and financial resources to prevent security issues. This relates to Pinto's (2018) discussion on issues with foreign technologies that are for-profit. Pinto (2018) talks of security threats when using technology from abroad, as these platforms want to connect as many people as fast as possible for profit: "when the critical infrastructure is provided by someone else, it is difficult to improve or enforce enhanced setting for privacy since the infrastructure and equipment is designed to serve the purpose of [different] countries". As these platforms want to connect as many people as fast as possible, for profit, they neglect issues of privacy ad security online. "when the critical infrastructure is provided by someone else, it's difficult to improve or enforce enhanced setting for privacy since the infrastructure and equipment is designed to serve the purpose of [different] countries". As Participant 30 from Gia Nghia says,

> We are now using only Youtube but our strategy is to find another channel more specialized and as a back up for Youtube. I can see that social networks allow huge freedom so the security and data security (of those platforms) are very complicated. A small enterprise or an enterprise operating in the arts will have huge difficulties to invest into improving (those platforms') security. I heard about what happened with the Youtube channel of Thanh Nien newspaper which has been hacked. That is a warning signal for those who invest hugely into Youtube. We have to be cautious. Participant 10 from Song Hong also mentioned their website had been hacked and that they were worried that content online including the archive could be lost: "these platforms are free but we have no control…one week before Covid, our website and Facebook went down due to hackers.

For instance, creating digital platforms in dual language can be difficult due to lack of technical, financial and human resources. As Participant 6 from Ky Cung says, "we don't have English on our website or Facebook and this is a limitation". They feel they have to build sites with dual language from the outset, but this is difficult because it takes more time, staff, money, and technical skills. As Participant 27 from Tay Ninh says:

> My website was launched in 2017. I am not yet happy with it. The design is ok, the content is rich. The only problem is with the language. Our website now is in English only. The limitation is there is no Vietnamese. Our website is customized and not developed on the basis of a template. It cost me hugely. To use template is very easy. But I want my website to be representative of the brand. It must be original and serves the purpose of telling the story of my brand. It cost a lot of money and took me 2 years. So as I finished the English version, I run out of money for the Vietnamese version. Our Facebook is dual languages.

The impact of these challenges is that they are hindering their ability to exploit technologies for high-quality digitization and to utilize digital platforms for display. Another dimension of the discussion on access is about cultural professionals' level of accessibility to good-quality technical equipment. This links to the technical challenges they face in digitization and how it impedes the quality of content they can produce. It is about having all types of platforms/techs at their disposal to choose from. Hence, these challenges are jeopardizing the digital transition of the cultural sector. The impacts of these include limited developments in digital platforms and in digitization. Also, the lack of human, technical, and financial resources impacts the rate of, quality of, and amount of digitization. Two respondents specifically mention the effects of the main challenges of human resources, technical resources and budget – being that it is impacting on limited developments in digital platforms and digitization. They cannot do as much digitization or/and utilize digital platforms as they would like or wish/aim for due to the country-specific challenges they face. As Participant 19 from Hai Duong says, "digitization is still very rudimentary, not professional enough, due to time, financial & human resource constraints". As Participant 15 from Thuy Khoi says

> We do things on the basis of availability of people and/ or money. If there is no personnel, or volunteer or money, we would not do anything… guerrilla warfare style, home-grown style, depending on the availability of personnel and platforms.

The tension here is that they are forced to be online and to digitize but in Vietnam there is not all the available resources they need in order to do it properly as well as the hidden challenges that make it more difficult. So some feel unsatisfied with what they can do/produce with the resources they have: As Participant 15 from Thuy Khoi says:

> if we don't upload things online, no one knows what we are doing. But if we want to do so, it is a huge burden. […]I always have a headache whenever I try to use my Instagram. It will be much better if there are more people who work in art sector and can provide extra support to those who are working in or managing creative organizations. More platforms require more people to operate them. […]After all, platforms are platforms. But in order to use them, we need resources, especially human resources.

Summary

This chapter reflects a digital transition in the culture sector in Vietnam, from creating digital copies for cultural preservation to creating publicly accessible resources for cultural presentation and promotion. However, there needs to be a lot more infrastructure and support in order to ensure effective digitization and development in the cultural industry. Furthermore, cultural professionals see these digital objects and virtual experiences no longer as surrogates and copies of the physical but, instead, as a way to provide new experiences and to create new meanings about art and culture. Digital content is desperately needed for education, international relations, and as soft power assets to showcase to the world.

There have been developments in cultural professionals' digitization practices. This has included the digitization of more types of art, including the digitization of their working process and trialling digitization with new types of experimental art. Artists have had to learn new skills to adapt to the online mode, where technical and spatial aspects are completely different from the physical environment. Curators or directors have also had to learn new skills in organizing online events and how to publish artworks on digital platforms. This has meant the inclusion of new aspects of their work and new types of artwork.

This new body of accessible digital content enables the audience to gain a much more comprehensive view of Vietnamese culture today. Furthermore, the audience can see the final products, events, but also their working practices and daily lives. As a result, digitization practices are resulting in the creation of a digital culture. The digital culture that is now being created reflects cultural professionals' motives for digitization. They wish to share a contemporary image of Vietnam, to share their story, to share diverse representations of Vietnamese culture, and address the imbalance in resources online. This shows the importance and value of digitization for making access, dissemination, and promotion of their culture. This chapter has also been about professionals' opinions about access. For them, access is about a balance of flows into and out of Vietnam. They feel this is crucial for creating meaningful access.

However, cultural professionals face challenges in digitization, such as the need for skilled professionals dedicated to this role and availability of technical equipment that can be used to properly digitize artworks, and the need for budget for doing this task properly with quality. Artists and cultural professionals face two different layers of challenges. There are country-specific, socio-economic challenges, including lack of human resources, technical resources, and budget. There are also global geopolitical challenges, in the form of disadvantages in access and inclusion in the discourse on art and culture online. This is exacerbated due to having to use global (Western) digital platforms, tools, and apps, with algorithms that have an innate bias towards content from the West, using 'terms and conditions' that reflect Western ideologies. This also includes deep-seated social inequalities Vietnamese cultural professionals face in terms of power relations due to a confluence of geography, language, race, history, and (mis)representation. For instance, these actors face difficulties with having to translate Vietnamese into English or in using dual language on social media as well as being represented by others through images of tourist hotspots and conflict. This is what can be termed as a geopolitics of route, pace, force, and friction in digitizing art and culture. Due to these challenges, much of their work projects or artworks are not being made publicly accessible to the highest quality nor at the quickest pace or to the extent they wish for and cannot expand their connections as far (internationally) as they would like.

Notes

1 The British Council operates in Vietnam since and provides assistance in developing the creative and cultural industries through funding projects. For instance, projects like Creative and Cultural Hubs 2018–2021 and Collab Partnerships between the UK and Vietnam in 2022.

References

Dan, N. (2018) "Developing Vietnam's Cultural Industry." Asia Views. February 23, 2018. https://Asiaviews.net/developing-vietnams-cultural-industry/

Ly, T. (2016) A Research Paper about Policy and Creative Hubs in Vietnam. British Council. https://creativeconomy.britishcouncil.org/media/resources/research-paper-about-policy-and-creative-hubs-in-vietnam.pdf

Ministry of Planning and Investment. (2016) 30 Years of FDI Mobilization in Vietnam: New Vision, New Opportunities in New Era. https://www.economica.vn/Content/files/PUBL%20%26%20REP/30%20Year%20of%20FDI%20in%20Vietnam.pdf

Ngo, L., V. Tran, and M. Tran. (2019) "A study on relationship between cultural industry and economic growth in Vietnam." *Management Science Letters* 9 (6): 787–794. https://doi.org/10.5267/j.msl.2019.3.009

Pinto, R. A. (2018) "Digital Sovereignty or Digital Colonialism?" *SUR International Journal on Human Rights* 5(2): 15–27. https://sur.conectas.org/en/digital-sovereignty-or-digital-colonialism/

Vietnam News. (2020) Digital Transformation in Việt Nam: From Aspiration to Reality. December, 17/2020–08:25. https://vietnamnews.vn/economy/829504/digital-transformation-in-viet-nam-from-aspiration-to-reality.html

Vietnam News. (2021) Việt Nam Targets Further Digital Transformation in 2022. December, 24/2021-17:07. https://vietnamnews.vn/economy/1109594/viet-nam-targets-further-digital-transformation-in-2022.html

Vietcetera. (2018) Cultural Trends in Vietnam: Five Experts Share Their Insights. https://vietcetera.com/en/cultural-trends-in-vietnam-five-experts-share-their-insights

3 Digitization and Digital Platforms in Practice

Introduction

This chapter focuses on examples of how cultural professionals are publishing and displaying art content on digital platforms, which includes curating artwork and exhibitions for digital spaces as well as sharing stories and messages. It explores how cultural professionals use digitized content to create exhibitions and events online, how they build digital communities around art, and how they showcase Vietnamese contemporary culture to national and international audiences.

This chapter includes specific examples of cultural professionals' use of digital platforms and apps to display artworks in new ways, for instance, with the use of VR and AR. It explores both the opportunities for the publication and accessibility of art for Vietnam but also, at the same time, the challenges of having to use foreign technology. Hence, one of the central questions of this book will be discussed in this chapter – whether this situation is creating more equal inclusion and meaningful access for cultural professionals or if it is exacerbating already existing forms of digital cultural colonialism.

As well as providing examples of use of digital platforms, apps and 360° virtual tours, this chapter also explores dominance of Facebook in Vietnam amongst both the general public and for work in the cultural sector. It will discuss the role of Facebook today in Vietnam for the presentation and exhibition of art and culture. It also shows why cultural professionals choose Facebook over websites and over the national platform Zalo by illustrating how Facebook can be used for immediate, live connection with the audience, and a multimedia medium or tool for publishing, dissemination, and presentation of cultural content and events. Moreover, being free and widely accessed makes it an easy choice for cultural professionals who face challenges with budget, staff, and lack of technical equipment. Facebook capitalizes on this need. This chapter shows particularly how they have harnessed and tailored Facebook over the past three years, from 2019 to 2023, for exhibiting art and culture and for creating local (professional and general) communities around art.

DOI: 10.4324/9781003352792-4

It is about their divided opinions on use of digital platforms. Contradictions sometimes as they know the opportunities but also share their concerns about using foreign and commercial plats. The chapter is also then about how they use different types of platforms for different types of work, including websites, apps, AR/VR, and social media sites.

However, this chapter also highlights how they face challenges with the use of digital platforms. For example, they have to use foreign technologies. In relation to Facebook, there are issues with image quality, search engine optimization (SEO), dual language, Facebook policies, and Facebook algorithms that keep on lowering their visibility. This reflects general issues with social media platforms in terms of controls and filters as well as how non-commercial content from small organizations and independents are not highly visible. These constraints should be taken into consideration as it is the main route to display, publish, and disseminate digitized art and for providing art experiences in Vietnam. This is important to consider as it determines what kind of digital culture is produced and how it is displayed online.

Divided Opinions about Using Digital Platforms

It is important here to state the nature of digital platform usage in Vietnam. As of January 2022, there are 76.95 million social media users in Vietnam. This is 78.1% of the total population. Facebook has 70.4 million users in Vietnam (Datareportal 2022), 91.7% of internet users in Vietnam use Facebook, 98.8% access Facebook via smartphones (Datareportal 2022), and 95.8% of users in Vietnam access the internet via a mobile phone (Datareportal 2022). This is often used over and above websites. As a result, the main route for publishing digitized content for professionals working in the cultural sector is via Facebook. Facebook is also the most commonly used digital platform amongst the general public in Vietnam. Additionally, Facebook is the most commonly used digital platform for work in the cultural sector. However, while there is also a national messaging app, Zalo, it is not as popular for work and is not conducive for publishing or sharing art and culture content – and, moreover, smaller national companies such as Zalo find it difficult to compete against the tech giants like Facebook. This shows how Vietnam contrasts with some countries where both professionals and audiences are leaving free social media platforms in favour of more professional and creative platforms that have high-quality image resolution and better organization of content.

Nevertheless, with cultural content and cultural experiences increasingly published and disseminated online via Facebook in particular in Vietnam, it is important to understand changes in how Facebook is structuring the publication and dissemination of digital culture. Today, the nature of what culture looks like on digital platforms is dependent on how Facebook is controlled and regulated. It is also important to consider whether their policies, values, and terms of service 'fit' with Vietnam, who is producing and publishing the cultural content onto the platform.

Facebook is becoming increasingly profit-oriented. Art spaces, galleries, and independent artists are negatively affected by these changes. During 2021 and 2022, Facebook has been making major alterations in how users' newsfeeds display content, moving away from organic reach so that more personal connections have visibility. However, these modifications are a strategy to generate more advertising revenue as an increasing amount of businesses are spending money to increase their visibility on Facebook. Conversely, this lowers the visibility of non-for-profit or not profitable arts organizations and artists, who do not pay Facebook for ad space and do not publish commercial content. Hence, they do not have the same ability to reach their audience and even less likely to attract new audience members who are outside of their existing friendship connections. As a result, they no longer have the same visibility as they once did on Facebook. More worryingly, these changes in Facebook could be leading to a more corporate-led digitization and display of culture. As a result, some cultural professionals feel they have to act more businesses-like on social media platforms. This is echoed by Yeo (2020), who asserts that social media sites have reconstituted cultural institutions into instruments for capital and further morphed and absorbed them into the marketplace.

These issues are reflected in the experiences of some Vietnamese cultural professionals. As Participant 27 from Tay Ninh says "as of now, interactions via Facebook are low because of their new policies". This can also be attributed to the increasing amount of published ad content, which creates more competition for the visibility of their pages. These issues with Facebook in needing to pay for better platform SEO and service is outlined by Participant 12 from Tay Ho, who says "the free stuff can only satisfy our needs at a certain level. For better results, we need to pay". The issues with visibility of their content and posts as well as Facebook policies always changing without any notice are expressed by Participant 15 from Thuy Khoi, who says

> if we do not post, then only people who hang out in this space or who meet and talk to me directly know. So people cannot see everything we do from Facebook. Facebook changes its policies a lot. There is no notice in advance for users and they just apply the changes on sight.

Algorithms mean users do not see everything but rather what Facebook algorithm thinks they will like based on previous behaviour, activity, and existing friendship groups. As Participant 15 from Thuy Khoi says "Social networks are run by algorithms. They will not offer us a menu of varied dishes but they customize in accordance with the content you have seen".

The concern is in Facebook's Terms of Service, which stipulates that "users grant Facebook a non-exclusive, transferable, sub-licensable, roy-alty-free and worldwide license to host, use, distribute, modify, run, copy, publicly perform or display, translate and create derivative works of your content" (Terms of Service, Facebook, 2022). In other words, they hold a lot of rights over how to distribute, copy, reuse the content, which basically gives them the copyright. However, Facebook decides how to target ads and rank content based on its algorithms. As a result, some cultural professionals feel they must publish frequently for any chance of increasing their visibil-ity. As Participant 26 from Bien Hoa says: "You have to update frequently. With or without changes in their algorithms, they still force us to update everyday". They will loose their position and visibility if they do not update frequently and consistently. Hence, they are dictated by the platform and its algorithms.

Facebook determines what the cultural professionals (working at art spaces or private galleries) or independent artists can do on their platform. For instance, Facebook determines image quality level. Participant 16 from Cam Thuy also says there are issues with image quality, saying "Facebook is not for archiving and the quality (of photos & videos) there is not high". Also, Participant 23 from Canh Ram says "the quality of photos posted on Facebook is lower than on the website".

The challenge with using digital platforms, which is shared by many cul-tural professionals, is that the platforms they use are located, designed, and operated abroad. This is the case for social media platforms, websites, and applications. There is a common feeling amongst cultural professionals that they do not have control over how their content is distributed or shown. In this respect, these platforms are structuring and controlling the display and presentation of digital culture. This is an example of a new form of digital colonialism, whereby tech giants have produced sophisticated algorithms that learn from existing content. Moreover, platforms are becoming increasingly commercialized, which puts a disadvantage on small non-commercial art organizations or artists. In addition, Vietnam is dependent on foreign tech-nologies that are Eurocentric or Western centric in their values.

As Participant 27 from Tay Ninh says:

> the programmers and coders for my website are all from Russia. Social media platforms I use are developed by American companies. This means that these digital platforms are almost non-localized. We use services offered by these platforms but we do not own them or have rights over them. In the future, these platforms might be tailored for users of each country or each country might introduce their own digital platforms. Then I would feel less worried because I no longer have to use services offered by a company from another country.

However, others just see digital platforms as tools to showcase *their own* work. As Participant 14 from Hai Dung says in relation to the AR Into Thin Air project:

> the server is located abroad. We pay the fee to keep the app available in both iOS and Android versions[...]It is not modeled on anything internationally[...]it's not a platform for me, it's a tool to do it. And we put our work, the local artwork for the local public space, so it is just a tool, whatever it is. We don't compromise [our ideas or projects for Google or Apple].

Other respondents also shared how they have harnessed digital platforms and, as a result, have become stand-alone spaces for exhibition and display of art and cultural content. During the past three years, from 2019 to 2023, Participant 13 from *Ben Hai* says "we try to make the digital space a real experiential space, with uploading more art and doing virtual exhibitions, tours, with the same feeling as with the event in person, take part and ask questions". Participant 5 from *Bac Giang* says "digital platforms have developed and now can become an exhibition space". Participant 17 from *Hue Ho* says digital platforms like websites have become "a virtual room for creative work[...] now that working space no longer remains physical. Covid forced us to adapt and reveal new possibilities of digital platforms". As Participant 17 from Hue Ho says "Artists' websites become their studios. They can have multiple websites, each as a virtual room for creative work. We usually visit the studios to see artist's work, but now it's digital now that working space no longer remains physical".

Also, some participants mention how they actively curate their online spaces. As Participant 29 from Di An says:

> As we work with quite a number of artists... first we share on several platforms like Facebook, Instagram and other art platforms. Secondly, we share by topics or by exhibitions...Then there are appropriate events which are relatable with our artworks or artists or a certain circumstance. We will also share them. Thirdly we go by topics of exhibition. An exhibition can feature a lot of artworks and artists. The content can be in various formats: short featured clips, video of artist working in their studios, interviews with artists, pictures, scanned images, etc. there are many formats we can work with.

As a result, these digital art spaces reveal new experiences, new meanings, and new insights and views into culture with these new types of and styles of arts communication, display of artworks, and online events. As Participant 17 from Hue Ho says, using digital platforms has "forced us to adapt and reveal new possibilities". As Participant 12 from Tay Ho says "the fact is that online performance actually opens up new possibilities[...]we also try storytelling and performance". As Participant 24 from Ninh Binh says "Digitization helps us not only to pass information but also to ignite new ideas".

This also means there is potential to redress existing stereotypes and biases online. Participant 25 from Cat Ba talks about the opportunity of digital platforms for presenting and sharing new viewpoints as well as updated perspectives on older topics like war – "I am optimistic that the world will attain different viewpoints because artists actively look for new ways of 'showing', they will address different viewpoints and diverse opinions".

As Participant 3 from Mong Cai says, "what I am starting to do now, by sharing the artworks and their stories, people can see a renewal of philosophies and mindset...I hope that the audience, both domestic and international, will start to see more than just artworks". This is possible because, as Participant 2 from Quây Son says, through giving access to and via publishing digitized content "on digital platforms, we are showing not just digital art but digital culture", meaning that people can also get a sense of the contemporary culture in Vietnam through sharing art online.

Virtual Exhibitions and Augmented Reality Apps

More art spaces and cultural centres in Vietnam are using virtual tours and 360° views alongside the physical exhibitions. However, this of course requires sufficient funding and technical support. Such 3D digital navigation tools allow wider possibilities for access to the exhibition, either through enabling the audience to experience the exhibition from home or through being able to use it at the exhibition in order to receive more information.

One example where digital technology provides more possibilities to show different sides of the culture is the virtual exhibition entitled "The Mekong, stories of man" by photographer Lam Duc Hiên from May to June 2021. This is a photographic narrative by the artist who travelled along 4,200 km of the Mekong river over 15 years. The photographs show the everyday life and culture along the sides of the river. Hiên combines his personal story (as he grew up next to the river) with issues surrounding what the future holds for the river as well as related international issues of cooperation, environmentalism, and modernization. Hiên's complex photographs manage to reflect on the past while also offering indications of the future. The benefit of using this digital platform is that there are also personal stories behind each artwork and photographs of the people who are involved in the cultural practices that are captured in the photographs as part of the exhibition. This provides in-depth information about the topics and themes related to the photographs. For instance, the cultural practices and traditions of contemporary Vietnamese culture. This exhibition can be accessed online via: https://my.matterport.com/show/?m=UYsq4feq4x8&sr=2.77,1.53&ss=27&fbclid=IwAR2Hv-cY7X-ALkg30a0NpBOpwsRgMAzNLazB7UI27fVQKJ2PT2bKYEGWrwe4. The

Matterport platform provides a 360° digital view of the exhibition, where the user can navigate around the exhibition via their smartphone or computer. This virtual exhibition was created using the platform Matterport, which is a 3D camera and virtual tour software platform, with Headquarters in California, USA. The physical location of the exhibition is at *L'Espace* in Hanoi, which is a popular venue for art and cultural events that is funded and owned by the French Institute.

Another example of use of digital apps in innovative ways, specifically to discuss topics in new ways (not allowed in physical exhibitions due to government restrictions), is the 'Into Thin Air' project, which was designed and led by Participant 14 from Hai Dung in 2018–2019. This project pushed the possibilities of digital platforms as it engaged different audiences beyond the traditional gallery walls. Furthermore, the artworks themselves were digital-born. The artworks was conceived as digital pieces by each artist. In this project, digital technologies are integral to all stages of the artwork production, from creation of the idea, filming, to the public's engagement via AR. They are displayed innovatively using an app and can be viewed using a smartphone with VR. There are stories and information on the app and there is audio and sound when viewing the works digitally on site. Importantly, these artworks are allowed in these locations because they cannot be seen with the naked eye; this also means the artworks can discuss themes that are not permissible in physical exhibitions. It is free to download and use the app and to see the permanent public art exhibition the spans across Vietnam's capital city, Hanoi, providing more opportunities for access to the art and its themes to a broader audience because it is in public, uses an app/smartphone, and is free. Participant 14 from Hai Dung (creator of Into Thin Air) says "I think it should be free for everyone and art should be free, and especially public art should be accessible for everyone". Digital platforms also allow the artworks to be shown permanently and without any restrictions on themes/content. In Vietnam, government permission is required for every exhibition. In this case, it is not needed as they are digital rather than physical artworks. As a result, the public can access more variety and diversity of contemporary art through the use of digital platforms.

Their developments in use of digital platforms also means they have experimented with digitizing new types of art, including contemporary performance and installation art. There are a total of ten artworks in this AR project Into Thin Air, which creatively explore contemporary issues of urbanization, commercialization, and loss of tradition.

As Participant 14 from Hai Dung says, they received a "small grant from Goethe institute and Dutch embassy but the major amount comes from UNESCO" to fund this project. "The project has attracted more than 20,000 visitors from different backgrounds, including young students, intellectuals, workers and artists of Hanoi" (UNESCO 2018). There have been "more than 30,000 downloads of the app, via IOS. All kinds of young but maximum 50 years old.

Just need to download from app store or google play" (Participant 14 from Hai Dung). This way, as Participant 14 says, they can "reach young audience who enjoy smartphones and love seeing things on high-tech apps". The audience can access the public art project via their smartphones, tablets, or iPads. The app and this type of technology in the art experience has attracted many people, providing and enhancing the level of engagement in Vietnamese art by choosing an appropriate type of technology for access and making it free for everyone. For Participant 14 from Hai Dung, effective publication of art via digital platforms is about making sure the art is accessible to the audience. This means making sure it can be accessed via smartphone apps and by putting the digital art into public spaces.

The contemporary dance performance "Remember the Times" by dance choreographer Vu Ngoc Khai was created using digital technologies. With this piece, the artist wants to highlight a forgotten and overlooked space in the city. With the AR dancers in front of the temple, the artist also asks the question of whether old and new can coexist. The artist also questions whether there is anything different today compared with the past.

'A Way to Preserve' by Nguyen Huy An is located in Lenin park (also known as Chi Lang Park). This is a popular public space in Hanoi. In 1985, the Vietnamese Government erected a 5.2 m bronze statue of Lenin. For Huy An, Lenin statue is part of the Hanoi scene and history in a similar way to other examples of Indochine architecture. For the past two years, Huy An has researched changes in the shadow of the sculpture following the sun and time of day at the park. His work for Into Thin Air is a virtual installation of twenty shadows of Lenin floating over the space. Since the statue of Lenin is in danger of removal, the artist wanted to preserve this historical icon by visualizing and digitizing it and keeping it in the cloud (the app technology) and ability to make it accessible via the digital app.

'From Below, Upward' by Nguyen Oanh Phi Phi is digitally displayed on a skywell of one of the big and oldest markets in centre of Hanoi, called Chợ H.m (Hom Market). It is about the increasing lack of unclaimed and non-commercial spaces in an urbanized city. With regard to this specific market, the piece also refers to the dislocation that labour migrants from rural areas feel in this urban life. Phi Phi Oanh utilizes the only disregarded space of the ceiling to create the image of a fish pond, projecting the gaze of the viewer from the urban setting into a nostalgic landscape. This resembles a fish pond or ao nhà, which has a symbolic place in village culture – triggering nostalgia for many Vietnamese people.

In addition, new digital technologies of AR and animation are being used to engage audiences in traditional Vietnamese art styles. For instance, some artists are using AR technologies to provide new ways of displaying and experiencing traditional Vietnamese art styles. For instance, Participant 28 from Ha Noi combines traditional lacquer painting with the new technique of AR. Participant 28 realizes the potential to engage audiences in traditional

Vietnamese art through the use of digital technologies. In order to view and access, the user must install an app, called Artivive, on their phone and open Participant 28's website on another device (laptop for example). The user must then open the app and scan the phone over the paintings on the website, in order to see the animation. Participant 28's Facebook page includes photographs of their lacquer paintings and use of digital technologies to make this traditional style more engaging for young audiences.

Similarly, Participant 26 from Bien Hoa uses AR technologies in exhibitions and filters on Instagram over the traditional Vietnamese art style of watercolour. In a similar way to Participant 28, access is about making digital content engaging for audiences for Participant 26.

> AR technologies are applied over my watercolor paintings to become a filter. People can turn on that filter while using Instagram and they will see the animals moving. That is how we try to digitize the traditional materials to make them appealing to the younger generations.
>
> (Participant 26)

The artist uses digital platforms to show the audience how they ready their watercolour paintings for digital animation technology. The artist applies AR technologies so that the viewer can see the digital animation over their watercolour paintings by using their smartphone, iPad, or computer.

Websites and Online Workshops

Over the past three years, from 2019 to 2023, there has been more use of digital platforms to hold art events. This of course became crucial during the Covid-19 pandemic. However, this has now become a common feature at many art organizations in Vietnam since the pandemic. Participant 7 from Thai Binh organizes and holds workshops on Vietnamese traditional art & famous Vietnamese artists. The workshops include examples of artworks like lacquer paintings at the Museum of Fine Arts in Hanoi and from artist Bui Xuan Phai. The course is delivered online and has a website: https://titoay.vn/course/truyen-thong-danh-hoa-viet/. This actively enables more available resources about Vietnamese art and culture to be published online and for educators, students, researchers, or the general public to access. Even though they must use foreign apps and platforms to host such events online, they are still able to then make these art events public and accessible. Participant 7 from Thai Binh says there is

> too much content from the West online for resources and not enough on Vietnamese art and culture [...] We want to have more resources available for students here about Vietnamese art and culture as more resources used come from the West [...] we want to teach more about Vietnamese art and culture and show Vietnamese artists are just as important as Picasso.

Moreover, their main goal with these workshops is to show Vietnamese people that their culture and history is just as important as Western culture. They feel that their culture should also be included and represented online. These workshops, therefore, do just that. Before 2019, they did these workshops in person, but online is a permanent record and resource for anyone to 'go to' and access.

Participant 8 from Thao has been doing many online workshops, they have received more interest in Vietnamese contemporary art and culture from Vietnamese population (before they did not value their own culture so much) and they have received more international interest in what they are doing. So in fact Thao now has more national and international connections. For example, the children's workshop Facebook project, with the aim to get the local community involved in art and then posting their creations on Facebook. It shows the community's responses to this moment, with a lot of visual references to the virus with spots and virus shapes. This is an example of innovative curation of content and inclusion of artworks by the general public. This event was held on Facebook and the results, which were sent in by the parents, were also subsequently published on Facebook. The images painted by the children show images of colourful virus shapes and buildings with spots inside. Participant 8 from Thao says "we continued to maintain connection with the audience by promoting a dynamic and creative spirit throughout organizing art events, like workshops and talks in the form of online, to help spread positive energy in the time of instability". As Participant 8 from Thao says "we tried to spread positive energy by sharing positive content including links to free online art course, art tours; encouraging people to be more creative and do new things with art". They chose to share posters and links to the workshops via their Facebook page, the most commonly accessed digital platform in Vietnam, so that the hope of the most amount of people to see and then decide to take part in the workshop.

The use of websites in Vietnam cultural sector is particular due to challenges in lack of human, technical, and financial resources. This makes Facebook an even more popular choice because it is free and easy to use. Most crucially, many cultural professionals do not yet have a complete or up-to-date website. Even for those who do, they are still developing it, or it is not yet in dual language, or it is not as up-to-date as they would like. For those who do have a website, it is used for posting formal information and storing archives, and not for immediate uploads and sharings. For one artist who does have a finished website, such as Participant 18 from Linh Duy, who has a complete public/accessible digital archive of all their 2D and 3D artworks along with commentary and media publications about their work, they say "Website is not interactive; it is mainly for information search; it is more stable, less versatile and it has to be accurate to be a long-term reference source". Participant 18's website is a permanent record and resource for contemporary art practice. It is also a permanent record and resource for accessing current-day themes and issues – such as urbanization, security, and poverty.

Other artists state particular affordances of Facebook in opposition to their website. As Participant 23 from Canh Ram says:

> I have been using Facebook for a long time. [...] The audience can reach me via Facebook, private messages and links shared on my Facebook. Facebook content is more instant [...] The way content is posted on Facebook is more instant, faster and more flexible. A website is more like a personal database and more serious.

Another artist who uses Facebook for its immediacy and casual friendliness is Participant 17 from Hue Ho, who says

> Pictures and videos shared on the website have to be very professional and well edited. Those shared on Facebook are more casual and sometimes unorganized. For example, I do a painting in the morning and, in the afternoon, the first draft is already on Facebook. So it is more friendly. [...] On the website there will be everything about my artworks: where they are made, their size, their material, their statement, the ideas behind. All photos there are of high resolution and downloadable.

There are some similarities in how some curators and directors feel about the different affordances of different digital platforms. As Participant 15 from Thuy Khoi recognizes, the website is official and serious while Facebook is an immediate, live view and for interaction:

> website is immobile platform [...] Facebook is more for communicating and exchanging information while the website is the official channel, the representing face of the essence of your organisation. [...] social networks offer us a real time view. Even the website is latent because we have to edit a lot. It might take us 1 to 2 years before we post something on the website.

Social Media Sites

There are particular reasons why cultural professionals choose Facebook as their main digital platform. They use Facebook for its ability to build local communities, for its immediate, friendly communication style, and for its interaction. As Participant 10 from Song Hong says, "Facebook is more interactive while website is more one-way interaction". Also, Participant 18 from Linh Duy says "Website and Facebook are two different mediums and the way we use them to reach the audience is also different. Facebook is flexible, updated with diverse art activities – both formal and informal". Friendliness and interaction provides a closer connection to the audience.

Facebook is useful for building local communities around particular art forms, such as around Vietnamese photography or contemporary fine arts. It is important to use common platforms to do this, as Participant 30 from Gia Nghia says,

> We use social network because, in principle, we are making arts for the community as a non-profit business. So we still need to have information channels for the popular community, for all groups of audience. No group must be excluded from accessing that information.[...]Those information channels are accessible for everyone.

Facebook is used more for connecting with the local audience, or for "connecting to the community" as Participant 30 from Gia Nghia says. This relates to discussion about the philanthropic efforts on Facebook by nonprofit organizations choose Facebook due to being conducive for community building and direct connection and due to being a suitable platform for nonprofits to facilitate community from the bottom-up in a friendly, unofficial manner on a common platform. This also relates to the idea about meaningful access, as cultural professionals choose the most commonly used platform in order to give access to the most amount of people and a platform for live interaction and can have a dialogue with the audience and professional art community. In turn, they can both build and connect local community.

The past two to three years, between 2019 and 2023, has seen an emphasis in using Facebook for supporting and maintaining local community, providing care and solace by using art and cultural content, and using Facebook for its direct, friendly, and informal style of interaction. These factors are important to make people feel closely connected to community and feel at ease with art content. They use Facebook for local communication and adapt to a local language for building and interacting with community. As Participant 15 from *Thuy Khoi* says, "our language changed because it had to be also a language of culture for local audience to connect with them effectively".

Facebook is conducive for crises such as the Covid-19 pandemic because it can be used to tailor content for particular needs and recontextualize content to timely issues/events/crises. This is seen particularly in relation to the Covid-19 pandemic where content was recontextualized in relation to the Covid pandemic information or messages of care and solidarity. For instance, this can be seen in the ways that cultural professionals changed their approach in tone and language to suit the current moment and specifically support the local community.

For example, in order to engage the audience and successfully promote their space they shared useful information, Facebook posts included announcement posters with information updates about Covid-19 measures, in line with Vietnam Government directives. Participant 8 from Thao published posts to share Covid-19 information updates. For instance, they announced that people should "stay home, stay safe" in an announcement image with closed windows from the inside, conveying the message to stay at home in order to stay safe. There is an accompanying post that says (in Vietnamese and then in English):

> The Corona virus pandemic has and is creating big changes in lives: inconveniences, disruptions, difficulties…but it also offers us the opportunity to live slower, spend time for ourselves, love more and appreciate the good things. These days, we hope you stay home and stay healthy, may you be optimistic and find joy. Thao will share interesting information about art, unique creations, creative ideas…hope to inspire and spread positive energy to you during this pandemic. Good things will come and we will meet again!
> #stayhomestaysafe
> #stayhomesavelives
> #stayhealthy #staypositive #staycreative
> (Participant 8 from Thao, Facebook Post, 9th April 2020)

Participant 14 from Hai Dung appealed to the local art community to use artworks on their Facebook page as escapism, as a tool to "run away" from the physical confines imposed during social distancing measures. This was the first time artworks had been used in this way, published as a form of care and therapy for the community. Posts provided inspirational messages to promote community well-being, such as "art can feed the soul" and "everything will be alright" (Participant 14 from Hai Dung, 16th April 2020). On Participant 14 from Hai Dung's Facebook page, artworks are curated into exhibitions or collections. They categorize and curate existing artworks into new collections, creating new themes and meanings, bringing existing artworks into new relationships and groupings to share particular stories and messages related to Covid.

> 'Art is the only way to run away without leaving home' – Twyla Tharp.
> This quote from Tharp best reflects our lives at this historical and brutal time! And we'd like to show you some works by our contemporary artists, hope this will bring the way for you to run away during this social distancing.
> We hope you are all safe and healthy!
> Meet soon, sure?
> #Hai Dung Team
> #contemporaryart
> #artinthetimeofcoronavirus.
> (Participant 14 from Hai Dung, Facebook Post, 12th April 2020)

For instance, Participant 14 from Hai Dung posts consoled their audience by sharing their own experiences and showing 'behind the scenes' views of the art space in quarantine, reflective of timely collective feelings and visually communicating the feel and atmosphere of the physical art space. Using self-taken photographs, and regular updates like this with episodic narratives like a diary, published for the first time on their Facebook like this in order to share their journey and experience and emotions of closing and being in lockdown. There were posts with self-taken photographs inside the art space looking out the open windows to the trees and sunshine outside. The post says "A beautiful winter day" (Participant 14 from Hai Dung, Facebook Post, 10th March 2020).

The art spaces also promoted local and international events via Facebook for the local audience and artists to take part in events or to watch content as well as to take up work opportunities in order to 'run away' from reality of pandemic. The art spaces were empathetic towards the local audiences' needs for resources to access from home and professional artists' needs for work opportunities. For example, there were "calls for projects" for professional artists with motivational posts to get Vietnamese artists involved in interna- tional events and projects. Participant 14 from Hai Dung puts out a call to say:

> For Vietnamese artist's attention!
> Opportunity to participate in Goethe Institute's artist-residence pro- gram in Leipzig, Germany. Deadline: March 31, 2020.
> https/www.goethe.de/ins/vn/vi/kul/sup/npe/pla.html
> #Goetheinstitute.
> (Participant 14 from Hai Dung, Facebook Post, 28th February 2020)

During the past two to three years, between 2019 and 2023, cultural profes- sionals have developed Facebook from what was a marketing billboard to an experiential exhibition and events space. Facebook was a signpost for cul- tural events in physical space but now Facebook is itself a cultural space. As Participant 16 from Cam Thuy says, "we use digital platforms for more than communication.[…]using online platforms to disseminate [artworks], to exhibit and display, not just to communicate information…Before I just share on Facebook our events and invite people to join". As Participant 8 from *Thao* says, they used Facebook before lockdown for "event promotion, visual post with photographs of the event to attract more people to *Thao*, news about *Thao*'s activities, user-generated content with quotes from the audience, and announcements of *Thao*'s opening times". As Participant 12 from Tay Ho says

> digital technologies can also be used as a language of storytelling, so that we can widen our language. There is the possibility to turn them into a real language of creative work to tell a story rather than just a tool, a medium.

We can start to see social media as spaces of cultural experiences and where official digital culture is produced, shared, and remixed. Facebook is now a curated space and environment for art content and events rather than a bill- board for cultural events in physical space. As a result, Facebook is now a stand-alone space of culture in its own right.

Summary

Digitization includes the important final stage of publishing cultural content into digital platforms. This is arguably the most important part of the digitization process. This stage is especially crucial in Vietnam as there are not yet many available resources about art and culture online yet. With addressing this issue, these digital resources could help educators, students, and researchers as well as for the general public to learn and understand contemporary Vietnamese culture. This chapter has shown examples of how cultural professionals are using digital platforms to make digitized content accessible and available online. This stage in the digitization process also needs to be supported and included in national policy in order to ensure it is something that can continue and be sustainable, effective, and long-lasting.

This chapter has shown how cultural professionals are now using digital platforms in innovative ways. Moreover, the content that they are publishing is being done in line with *their own* way, with their own messages and creation and distribution of their own content. They have tailored digital platforms for their own needs and cultural values. This links to discussion in the previous chapter on the need for a self-determined image of Vietnam. Together, these developments in the use of digital platforms for contemporary visual arts communication pave the way for more effective – i.e. culturally relevant, localized, and time-specific – arts communication in the cultural sector. Today, digital platforms can become spaces of culture rather than only signposts for cultural events in the physical environment.

Contemporary visual arts communication via digital platforms in Vietnam is now about using digital media to produce audience-focused cultural interactive experiences, creating more community-centred experiences that reflect the value of community cohesion and sharing emotion. As a result, these developments could see digital platforms as more viable platform for professionals art communication and work in the future. In Vietnam, developments specifically on Facebook are important in communities and countries (like Vietnam) where Facebook is the most popular digital platform.

A lot of the discussion in this chapter has shown how cultural professionals have developed Facebook for the publication of artworks and cultural events. They have transformed Facebook into a space for culture rather than a billboard of adverts for culture in physical events. Facebook is conducive for this because it can create local community. Therefore, it became the main choice for professionals and the general public during the Covid-19 pandemic, because it helped them to maintain their community and support for local community. They have harnessed and tailored Facebook for its conduciveness to certain aspects of their practice, which were to be community-orientated, immediate, flexible, interaction, and live connection. This relates to discussion on digital empowerment in Chapter 1 but, at the same time, this also shows the importance of the medium as the means to publish art today. This shows the relevance of discussion also on digital colonialism in Chapter 1.

In particular, cultural professionals have managed to recontextualize Facebook during the Covid-19 pandemic, which shows how they have harnessed and tailored this digital platform for their specific needs. For instance, with the sharing of personal photographs of their own art spaces 'in quarantine' in order to maintain connection with their audiences. They applied a culturally and timely specific 'rhetoric of care' in order to connect to people on a more emotional level. Their caring rhetoric in messages and visual content reflected Vietnam's response to the Covid-19 pandemic, which was in accordance with an ethics of care that emphasized solidarity and responsibility towards the community. As a result, this provides a more personal but also deeper knowledge of the culture and arts practice. Thus, this provides more comprehensive access to Vietnamese culture. It is not only showing event announcements and adverts, as was the case in the past. Instead, Facebook is now used to showcase actual artworks, audience content, and their own personal photographs. Facebook is also used for not only final artworks but also cultural professionals' process.

These developments in use of digital technologies in the cultural sector have provided a more widespread acceptance and validation of digital platforms as a legitimate tool for work in the cultural sector and for the display and experience of art and culture. Hence, it identifies a viable digital solution for the future of work in the cultural sector and identifies opportunities of digital platforms for arts and culture digitization and publication. It also helps legitimize and show how digital platforms can be spaces for the production and circulation of digital culture – within the professional cultural sector and not only for amateur content. These developments in digital work can be taken forward into work practices in the future.

However, they are pressured to use the most popular platform for the audience in Vietnam and a superpower, which obviously has larger geographic and demographic reach than national platforms like Zalo. Furthermore, Facebook has an influential position in controlling publication, dissemination and curation of culture (i.e. how it looks and how it is shared) on the platform. This is reflected in how cultural professionals discuss issues of SEO, algorithms, policies, pressure to post every day. They also have concerns of dual language and image quality. The amount, quality, pace/rate of what they can do or have to do on Facebook is dictated by Facebook policies, in these respects. It is also partly the platform algorithms that mean stereotypes and global inequalities still persist online, because it is only this ad click data it works on, which may relate to things like Vietnamese tourist hotspots/traditional culture. This shows the control of these platforms over the creation and dissemination of culture.

We can no longer talk about access as a binary of 'have' or 'have not' as so many people now have access to the internet. This develops the discussion on access, as here we have delved more deeply into what access means for cultural professionals. It has shown how technology provides communities of practice in the Global South with a utility and access to information. However, more importantly, it provides them with a way to present their culture online. Instead, access is about more deep-seated, hidden, nuanced, longer-term issues around inclusion and existing cultural, geographical inequalities and geopolitics. It is also about what constitutes meaningful access for cultural professionals. It is about whether the producers of culture content online – directors, curators, artists – have access to platforms, technologies, equipment, and funding. The question is whether they have good enough access for enabling cultural professionals to be able to equally or properly participate in (the production of) the global discourse on art and culture. Hence, this has broadened discussion on access from user side or about providing only basic technical infrastructure to the Global South.

References

Datareportal. (2022) Digital 2022: Vietnam. https://datareportal.com/reports/digital-2022-vietnam

UNESCO (2018) Re|shaping cultural policies: advancing creativity for development, 2005 Convention global report, 2018. https://unesdoc.unesco.org/ark:/48223/pf0000260592

Yeo, S. (2020) "Access Now, But for Whom and at What Cost?" *Information, Communication & Society* 23(4): 588–604. https://doi.org/10.1080/1369118X.2018.1529192

4 Future Prospects and Concerns for Vietnam's Culture Sector

Introduction

This chapter provides foresight on future prospects and concerns for Vietnam's culture sector. In order to do this, this chapter shares cultural professionals' visions for the future of the cultural sector in Vietnam. This sheds light on the future needs and requirements for the sector that are needed for their ambitions to be possible. Their needs for the culture sector's digital development include enhancing and enforcing intellectual property (IP) protection and copyright laws, creating a national digital culture policy, and creating common standards and professionalism amidst a predominantly DIY culture of practice. It will also share their future ambitions, which can only be achieved after their requirements are met. Their ambitions include more cross-sector collaboration, international connections, sharing more diverse range of topics and viewpoints due to the democratic potential of digital platforms amidst censorship laws in Vietnam for physical exhibitions, and the creation of a national archive for *contemporary* Vietnamese art.

This chapter will assess the future of Vietnamese professionals' digitization practices. This includes discussion about what will happen to digitization practices post-Covid. The pandemic led to more pressured digitization as there was an emergency response to a crisis and an immediate full migration to online work. Here, a question will be posed: what will post-Covid work look like? Many are talking about hybrid digital-physical models as a sustainable future for digitization. There is also discussion about seizing this moment when the world is more interested in the South East Asia region and when art galleries, fairs, and spaces around the world are more inclined to include artists from anywhere in the world due to holding events in online mode. However, they also share a sense of dissatisfaction because they cannot produce high quality content as in other countries.

The chapter will finally consider the future for Vietnamese art and art practices. This will foreground the new forms of art and art practices that are starting to come about as a result of the shift to digital work in the cultural sector. Hence, it will show the outcomes of the shift to digital, including how artists are

DOI: 10.4324/9781003352792-5

changing their entire practice and their artworks to suit digital display. This also means digitization is becoming an artform in itself. With this, we must be mindful that these digital platforms are for-profit and are commercially driven. This chapter will finish by considering whether this will jeopardize non-commercial arts endeavors and whether this will affect the aura and authenticity of art.

Future Needs for Digital Development

Cultural professionals want to ensure sustainable and effective digital developments in the cultural sector. First, they want to make the cultural sector more professional in its digital aspect, with training for artists, developing IP law, creating better enforcements for copyright infringement, creating a national digital culture policy, and creating a common set of standards. For example, there is a need for a digital culture policy to establish common standards so that professionals digitize by the same standards. As Participant 10 from Song Hong says, "there is no policy on digitization". Cultural professionals share a wish for a national set of rules on how to digitize and display content (including which technologies to use, which quality level content should be, and which platforms to use). This could be used by anyone and shared across the sector. In addition, content could be interoperable, meaning that their individual content could be placed on one common platform, it could be used across platforms, and it could be used by different people or organizations.

There is also a need for training resources that could be accessible to everyone online. Currently, cultural professionals say that they are unsatisfied with having to learn everything themselves. As Participant 9 from Lieu Giay says, support from the State is needed to "introduce training programs for artists and cultural managers in applying digital platforms in artistic practices". There is discontent from some cultural professionals towards the State for their lack of support and funding for the contemporary art scene. As Participant 9 from Lieu Giay says, "I think there must be official support from the State to introduce technical, financial, and promotional support for art projects involving digitization". There is a tension here because while they want to be free from any more top-down regulations, they also ask for more support to help them in their digitization projects.

It is important to creating a sufficient IP law that is enforced. As Participant 21 from Sun Tam says, "the official mechanism of copyright protection is ineffective". As Participant 10 from Song Hong says, "IP and copyright is an issue, which needs to be enforced by government and make the rules clearer". This would mean that professionals, including artists and art space directors, would feel more confident to publish artworks online as, at the moment, there is a fear of copying. This makes some decide not to publish some works or to publish artworks at a purposefully low quality. Some feel display is too risky due to copyright infringements not being enforced in Vietnam. They also have concerns about how people can easily download, share, copy their content without permission, which breaches copyright and, overall, decreases the value to art and artists. As Participant 8 from Thao says, "production and consumption of art online is easy and accessible but relaxed and unprofessional. There should be strategy in this".

The past three years have seen development in cultural professionals' strategies for digital content creation and display. A weakness is that these strategies are DIY and disparate as everyone is making their own. As Participant 23 from Canh Ram says, "in Vietnam now things are fragmented". There are yet to be standards and protocols and common platform or common training for this sector. As Participant 22 from Lang Son says, "each organisation has their own strategy of development and digitization". Vietnam's culture sector requires sufficient policies and standards in place in order for digitization and digital display to be done in a systematic, sustainable way (Duester 2021). As Participant 23 from Canh Ram says, "we haven't managed to do it in a systematic way. This requires efforts from the whole political, educational and cultural system". They also share about how government needs to realize the importance of and therefore support more this aspect of work and digitization concerning access. As Participant 22 from Lang Son says, "there is a need for more backing and support in the aspect of access".

There are many who stress the need for more professionalism amidst a predominantly DIY culture of practice. They have to do many things by themselves as they go through digital transition. This is not efficient or sustainable as everyone has to learn everything themselves. As Participant 24 from Ninh Binh says, "It is difficult to have extra support…I must teach myself". They share how they cannot rely on an agency, body, or the State for help. Participant 23 from Canh Ram says "there is little public sharing on how to digitize. There is also no organization, no state agency or groups to provide support". This has led some institutions to create their own copyright procedures. As Participant 29 from Di An says,

> how to protect the photos' copyrights all requires knowledge. In Vietnam, there is no agency which provides such support. Even we have to internalize all those services from the first until last step. So, of course, we have to take measures to protect our copyright.

Each institution is in charge of their own policies, protocols, and standards of practice. As a result, this means many are doing their own digitization practices and duplicating several of the same things. They ask for standards so that everything can be more streamlined and standardized.

In addition, they work amongst themselves within the art community, building communities amongst themselves to survive. Still, they realize that they need outside support and training from the State or other agencies. As Participant 21 from Sun Tam says "I only make videos when people I know are free to help". As Participant 28 from Ha Noi says, "we share resources.

We lend and borrow equipment to and from other artists. So we come together in communities to reuse those items. That is how we create opportunities for ourselves". For others, they rely on their family and friends. For Participant 28 from Ha Noi, they rely on friends as project partners to do the technical side or to sell artworks internationally:

> for my first working with AR technology, I partnered with a friend. That friend is in charge of technology aspects [...] most of my connections are via my extended family. I find it easier to sell my artworks via my family network.

As Participant 24 from Ninh Binh says, "one of my friends has his wife's help with preparing and posting on Facebook". This shows how a lot of developments and initiatives in the culture sector are happening from the bottom up, by individual artists and non-governmental art organizations. However, this is not a sustainable solution for long-term digital development.

Future Ambitions for Digital Work

Cultural professionals share their future ambitions for work at their organizations and for digital development of the cultural sector overall. There is a common sentiment for an increase in importance of making content accessible online but in the right way, with effective digitization. Participant 9 from Lieu Giay knows that "having the perspective of 'simply upload and it will be fine' is not enough anymore". Instead, they aim for digitization with curation and consideration. They want to ensure that everyone and each institution carries out effective digitization. Some mentioned that they would create a specific digital strategy, which they had not done before, to focus more on their digital work and to be more strategic and systemic about this, in order to ensure effective digitization practices. As Participant 1 from Phò Dày says, "this year we will make a digital strategy".

There is also a feeling amongst many cultural professionals that there needs to be cross-sector collaboration in order to develop effective and sustainable digitization. They feel the sector needs to pool resources from other industry sectors in order to be more professional and sustainable. Some said there needs to be collaboration with the digital sector, in order to overcome the challenge in human, technical, and financial resources. Participant 11 from Hian says "collaborating with dig sector is a must" in order to overcome challenges and to see the sector develop. Participant 1 from Phò Dày also says "we need to collaborate more with digital sector". A few are starting to work with the digital sector, as with Participant 14 from *Hai Dung* and Participant 1 from Phò Dày with digital art archive projects for contemporary art. However, they also shared experiences of difficulties with working with the tech sector.

In the future, cultural professionals want to forge more international connections. This is because they can collaborate and develop projects internationally, source funding, and introduce more people to Vietnamese contemporary art. As Participant 10 from Song Hong says, "we want to build more international connections". As Participant 11 from Hian says, "we have always prioritized international connections. This is central to our work day-to-day and central to the mission of the space. But we want to develop more international links". As Participant 7 from Thai Binh says, "we want to communicate with audiences internationally more in future and our hope for the future is to collaborate internationally with art centers". As Participant 1 from Phò Dày says, their future plan is to "find more ways to connect internationally". Others like Participant 30 from Gia Nghia want more international connections in order to forge more partnerships:

> now we start to have international partnerships. We have established connection with a network of the biggest art organisations and galleries in the world. Besides, we are conducting international market studies with some European countries. Some investors are expressing their interests in our gallery and they contacted us. There is one such investor from UK.

Many want to educate the Vietnamese population using the body of digital content they have now created. They wish to do this via social media, workshops online and hybrid digital-physical exhibitions in their physical space, or by using digital content as a digital resource in school and university curriculum or other educational programs. They want to update the Vietnamese population's understanding of art from associated with propaganda being seen as something that is accessible for everyone, contemporary, and exciting. As Participant 11 from Hian says, "we want to create more links with Vietnamese ppl to show them art is open and contemporary. As our mission and message is to educate Vietnamese". They also wish for contemporary art to be taken seriously by the State and seen as professional. With this, it can become part of national education syllabus and respected by the State in the same way as cultural heritage. Cultural heritage and traditional culture have been prioritized in Vietnam for funded preservation projects. However, digitizing contemporary art and culture is important alongside the preservation of cultural heritage as it can be displayed today on digital platforms to show Vietnam's contemporary culture. This can also engage young audiences in Vietnam and abroad to understand art and understand contemporary Vietnamese culture. Hence, the history of Vietnam is significant to understand the current state of digitization and development of the cultural sector. As Participant 10 from Song Hong says, it is a "communist country where art and culture traditionally used for and perceived as propaganda". As a result, people in Vietnam are often scared to visit museums and galleries because they see art as propaganda and linked to the State. This can change if there is a move towards changing the way people think about art. This can be done with use of contemporary art with new, creative interactive digital content on popular digital platforms. Participant 9 from Lieu Giay says "the Vietnamese audience are more responsive to artworks on digital platforms. They must be provided with detailed information and guidelines for their experiencing. Otherwise, artworks will remain inaccessible to the audience".

Some also specifically state the need for an online archive for specifically contemporary Vietnamese art. They want an archive that is open-access and centralized. This is in contract to what is happening today, as they say, that is fractured with many disparate digital collections and digital archive work going on. For instance, Participant 1 from Phò Dày is doing one part at their organization, who says "we are developing content for online as we want to create a national online archive. There is a selection and curation for the archive – based on location, discipline, region, time period". The main long-term goal of many cultural professionals is to have a national digital archive for contemporary Vietnamese art and culture that is accessible to everyone. As Participant 10 from Song Hong says, "there is a need to have a digital archive for Vietnamese art and culture". As Participant 14 from *Hai Dung* says,

> we lack a professional art archiving system [...]. So, it will be difficult for people to access, for outsiders to gain a comprehensive view [...] As a result, it is a great pity that young Vietnamese has almost no opportunity to access to art.

The Future of Digitization Practices amidst Issues with Access and Inclusion

Today, there is more pressure around access and inclusion. The Covid-19 pandemic has made the global disparity in terms of levels of quality more visible. This is because the general public can access all content online and compare its quality very easily, highlighting the fact that Vietnamese cultural professionals cannot produce high-quality content due to lack of resources. This issue has been exacerbated because of the reduced amount of resources during the pandemic. As a result, some cultural professionals feel pressure to digitize more and quicker. There is pressure to digitize cultural content and make it public because organizations in other countries are doing more due to the global acceleration in digital work in the cultural sector, which was brought on by the Covid-19 pandemic and will continue now into the future. This makes some Vietnamese professionals feel pressure to digitize and publish because they do not want to be left behind or forgotten because of not being visible or 'existing' online. Some say there is no choice today and this situation pushed them to make everything public online. For instance, Participant 21 from Sun Tam says

> if you do not digitize, there is no other platform for you to show your works. People will not know what you are doing. Actually, there is no

choice but to make everything public [...] it pushed me to bring my artworks to digital platforms.

In addition, there is an increasing amount of high-quality content online. Some examples of regional contemporary digital art exhibitions include Singapore Art Week (SAW) 2023 that uses the platform ARTualize to create virtual exhibitions for each artist participating in SAW. The UCCA Center for Contemporary Art in Beijing, China, has created an immersive and interactive digital art exhibition called 'Animistic Imagery', based on a collaboration with Baidu and the Moment Factory to create an exhibition based on AI. By contrast, Vietnamese cultural professionals have had to adapt their ideas and aspirations to fit the level of available technologies, budget, and available staff. This leaves some to feel "dissatisfied because we cannot make the developments we would like because of lack of resources" (Participant 1 from Phò Dày).

However, the opportunities of the web for access and inclusion as well as for free from censorship in Vietnam are prominent. Some cultural professionals feel digital technologies and digital platforms as equalizing and democratizing, which is especially important in a communist country. This means cultural professionals can show contemporary art online without as many restrictions and censorship as is the case in physical spaces.[1] But we also must be mindful that Facebook also has strict censorship regulations, preventing a lot of contemporary art from being shown. As Participant 10 from Song Hong says, there is an "importance of historical context of Vietnam" (as a communist country where art has been propaganda) that means there are "opportunities of the internet in a communist country for democracy". This makes digital technology even more important because can be democratizing and freeing. As Participant 14 from *Hai Dung* says in relation to Into Thin Air project: "the reason for making it entirely digital is to avoid censure, so that we can benefit from democracy in creative work with no censure nor control on content and ideas". For them, there is a democratic nature of online as more voices can be included, the possibility to share more topics and viewpoints, and greater reach for their content. Even though they mention how online provides them with more freedom, democratic space, and open space, other respondents such as Participant 11 from Hian and Participant 10 from Song Hong say that a challenge with using online is censorship, which still prevents them from publishing everything they would like to display online.[2] This means there are still some barriers in access and inclusion due to national censorship laws. This leaves some feeling dissatisfaction as this will have lasting long-term effects on their ability to be included in global discourse on art and culture online. For instance, Participant 11 from Hian says "a challenge is censorship, as the gov still surveys Facebook". Participant 1 from Phò Dày also says that "even online some things are not allowed". Even though digitization has the potential to provide freedom and agency and voice, these profs still have to work within the remit of national policy. They are restricted in one respect by global, Western tech platforms as well as, in another respect, by national censorship. So overall there are mixed feelings about the future of digitization practices, as while it can allow more inclusion there are still some restrictions that they as Vietnamese need to consider.

Moreover, a few have realized that they need to seize this moment when the world is interested in the SEA region and when online makes people think about including artists, art galleries, and art spaces from anywhere in the world. Participant 20 from Long Cai says "Covid makes exhibition organizers realize that, to display their exhibitions, the paintings of artists from Hanoi or Saigon or Thailand or America is indeed the same. Geographic divisions become blur during the pandemic". Cultural professionals around the world are interested to do new things and bring in artists from different countries because more is online now, making it simpler to invite international artists or organizations to participate. This could last into the future, with more interest in the region. Generally, people realized that the digital means we can see new things or new parts of the world and audiences were encouraged to access new content. Vietnam could capitalize on this new interest brought about by the pandemic. As Participant 20 from Long Cai says, "there is a bigger interest in our region. Before the pandemic, there is little interest in the region. But now people are stay home more, they are curious to learn other things". Also, Participant 22 from Lang Son says

over the past few years, the area of sea has received much attention from world. Organisations from Europe and East Asia are oriented towards the SEA area. This opens up new and easier opportunities for partnership and exchanges than before.

The Future of Vietnamese Art and Art Practice Post-Digitization

The past five years have seen many changes in artistic practices and the nature of 'cultural work'. In addition, many aspects of work and practices in the cultural sector have become digital. For curators and art managers, they have had to create new types of digital content and digital spaces for exhibitions and events. Meanwhile, artists have had to adapt their artworks to suit digital display. For instance, Participant 21s artworks and work style have changed and have become more digital-focused:

it changed the direction in which my artwork is conceived and developed. Instead of making a costume to be worn for a live performance in a theater, I have to create a costume to stay still and to be remodeled on a digital platform. This means that the process of conceiving the artwork will take a different turn because of digitization of the physical artwork.

For Participant 21, the entire nature of their art practice is changing because all aspects need to be suitable for digital platforms. Also, Participant 9 from Lieu Giay talks about their digital focus for the future:

> I will move to the new field of applying AI and machine learning in com-posing and performing [...] Now I am preparing to compose new artworks in line with these targets. I hope I will have enough resources to introduce them to the audience.

Cultural professionals say the future should be based on a hybrid physical-digital approach to be sustainable. Some talk about sustainability in relation to digitization and how this needs to include a hybrid model in order for physical spaces to remain feasible, cultural profs can keep their job, and visitors still come to the physical spaces. As Participant 1 from Phò Dày says, "we have been thinking about how to be sustainable in the future". Several discuss using digital and physical in a hybrid format as a sustainable way forward. One hundred percent digital is not the answer for the future longevity of the sector, which means it is important to find suitable ways to combine both physi-cal and digital together. As Participant 22 from Lang Son says, their future approach will be "a combination mode of online and offline. We strive for an adequate ratio of combination".

Digitization is now central in art practice, and therefore *is* part of the art in itself. It is an artform of digitally documenting, recording, preserving, and digitally publishing. These individual professionals are using technologies, such as cameras and their smartphones, apps, VR, digital platforms, to docu-ment their daily working lives, their stories, their ideas, and to create and show artworks. Collectively, when this is altogether published and accessible online, it becomes digital culture – a collective body of digital work that is created by individual cultural professionals and independent artists. This digi-tal culture continuously changes and is reflective of each moment in history. For instance, digital platforms are now living archives or spaces of contem-porary culture. On these platforms, we can see the incremental and abrupt changes in culture and in how these art spaces share, comm with the use of art and culture to their audiences. What we see as the audience is evident with this content over time is changes in culture, mindset, and values. It is now more than just seeing artworks and information about artworks.

This is the future of digital content and experience. This is separate and different from the physical space. Digital platforms in themselves can now become part of digital culture. The practice and process and final products they share also become an artwork in itself. This is now a new form of cul-ture in itself, now a viable way of documenting contemporary culture with new meanings and new ways of experiencing it. Digital platforms allow them new ways of showing art and new digital modes of showing. As a result, there are possibilities for new meaning to be made with art, for new stories or new sides of the culture (not yet seen online), and for new types of art to be shown in new ways. This is not a copy of the original or physical version. This means that the use of digital technologies and digital platforms changes art. This emphasizes how 'effective digitization' in uploading and publishing is not just about putting an image online. There is currently a realization that digital platforms can provide new experiences and meanings that are different to physical space and that in future digital content needs to provide something different to the physical in order to be sustainable and last long-term.

With so much more content now online and more competition to be 'visible' and to increase SEO, there is a fear that in the future content will become more commercial. This is especially a concern for Vietnam as cultural professionals have no choice but to rely on Western commercial social media platforms that are free and commonly used. There are concerns about Facebook for the future of non-commercial endeavors, for the future of the meaning of art, and for communities in Global South producing and managing culture on digital platforms. There are concerns around the production of digital culture via Western platforms for communities in the Global South because many aspects are at odds with cultural values and ethics. Additionally, the problem is that such non-commercial content is not made highly visible by Facebook algorithms so perhaps the future will see more commercially orientated content. They have a powerful role as gatekeepers and mediators of culture, governing the creation, curation and presentation of digital culture. These digital platforms and technologies should remain as tools to be used by whomever wishes, so that each individual from whichever location, can upload and publish content in their own way. On one hand, digital transition and increasing use of digital platforms does enable new types of content to be easily uploaded and published, knowledge to be easily and widely shared and disseminated, and more diversity of voices to participate in the online discourse on art and culture.

Furthermore, due to all this original art content now newly displayed on mostly for-profit platforms, we see more of a merging or blurring of art and advertising. For example, this is the case on social media in particular. In addition, many art organizations have introduced new types of promotion that are more about social good as well as about promoting cultural experiences and about promoting their own space. With this introduction of more types of promotional content there is now a closer synergy between art and promotional content, reinforced by the way all posts applied a rhetoric of care during the Covid-19 pandemic. We see this perhaps here with a rhetoric of care that is perhaps a strategic way to promote their art space. So now there is no clear dividing line between original art, promotional content and advertising. This means that it could be more difficult for the audience to distinguish between art and advertising content. They perhaps feel they have to turn this way because it is a for-profit platform and this is the only way to gain more visibility and because the pandemic even more squeezed their budget and resources so have had to resort to more promotion. Some implications of this are that these digital spaces become more commercially driven and looking. Not only the pandemic, but the platform itself also makes these art spaces be more commercially minded in their posts on Facebook. So then we gain a commercial style digital culture now and future. The other implication is the lost of aura and authenticity of art itself. In addition, this brings a worry for the future of digital culture, that maybe will become more commercialized. As these digital platforms include both advertising of events as well as art itself. So both are increasingly becoming blurred. This may jeapordize the future of arts-centred work on for profit platforms.

Importance lies now in how cultural professionals use this digital culture that they have created in terms of what the future will hold. Will it be used for commercial purposes, showcasing their culture to the world? Will it be used for education purposes to put into schools and university curriculum for the next generation to learn from and to understand the value of their own culture? Overall, these decisions will determine the route of cultural sector development, but also how the next generation views contemporary art, its value, their way of access/inclusion in the global discourse on art, how they participate in the art world, and how the world sees contemporary Vietnam.

Summary

Together, this chapter has provided an analysis from cultural professionals in the sector on what is required in the cultural sector for development during digital transition, such as a common digitization policy and a set of common standards and protocols for all professionals to follow in the process of digitizing culture to ensure its sustain, profess, and that it is at an internationally competitive standard. It has achieved its aim which was to be relevant for industry and academics across South East Asia as well as developing countries as a useful resource to understand the pitfalls and how to overcome them. It has also been useful for those in Europe and America in order to understand more about how a developing country in Asia is starting to digitize and display its culture online.

There is a need for discussion about the value of creating digital cultural heritage in relation to digital inclusion and cultural equity for communities in the Global South. This chapter has provided a critique of the needs, requirements of cult profs in the digitization process. This will in turn develop the cult sector. For example, lack of policies and common standards are stifling the amount, pace, quality cultural professionals can do and impeding developments in the cultural sector nationwide. They face both tangible challenges and hidden geopolitical challenges. These challenges include the lack of human resources in terms of skilled personell, lack of funding, and lack of technical resources such as 3D scanners in order to properly digitize cultural objects. There is a need for more advanced digitization technologies, such as

3D scanners and 3D cameras, as well as a tech sector to be more experienced in this type of work. There are also other more hidden challenges that intersect the abovementioned challenges, like existing stereotypes, biases in platform algorithms, platform policies, using dual language. This shows how acutely these cultural professionals face precarities with digital inclusion and inequalities in their work.

While digital technologies allow VN cult profs to be more fairly included with their own voice, and for their work to be more easily accessible to audiences/cult profs elsewhere, these technologies also provide new types of hurdles and barriers. It is important to understand these issues in order to prevent further digital inequalities and a continued silencing of their voices in the future. That said, cultural professionals in the Global South are now more included and have more meaningful access to discourse due to digital technology. As a result, they are now more-so using digital platforms as tools for *their* content. Digital culture is importantly being created *by them* in ways that are important to them, relevant to aspects of their cultural values but also showing how they are same as world too. This aspect of culture, of knowing the world, from a Vietnamese perspective, or just more non-Western perspectives are needed in the digital space. These individuals and organizations have the power to show their culture with the use of digital technology. Moreover, they are documenting their process as well as conveying their own broader message about culture. This can also help institutions in Vietnam going through this now or other institutions in other countries. Vietnam is unique because it is in contrast to many countries across the world that have already passed this stage, without any documentation of it, but at same time, this investigation can allow other countries to reflect on the transition they have gone through. The case study on Vietnam can be useful for countries and sectors that are already advanced and through this stage that Vietnam is currently going through. It is also an import resource for other developing countries that are also now going through this process of transition. Yet, it is important to capture what is happening in the moment because we can learn from this and have it documented before the world moves on and forgets.

The disparity and inequalities here are to do with the fact that a lot is produced by the West on Vietnamese culture and the fact that a lot of Western materials are published and circulated online in comp to Vietnamese resources. This means educators for instance cannot find Vietnamese resources to teach with. The lack of resources online on Vietnamese art and culture has become increasingly evident with the global digital transition in the cultural sector. Digitization and digital display on digital platforms can allow increased inclusion of more non-Western aesthetic perspectives and help to address the current inequalities in the amount of accessible content online as well as the disparities in access to high-quality technical equipment, staff, and funding, as well as disparities in the control of production and circulation of cultural content online.

Overall, the has filled a gap in the literature on digitization, in terms of providing more analysis and discussion on the routes, motives, pace, and frictions during this process, as well as how cultural professionals digitize their artwork, what they choose to digitize and why, and their motives for providing a more diverse, contemporary image of Vietnamese culture and to provide more available resources for educators and researchers. Together, this demonstrates how digitization practices have become an increasingly central aspect of cultural professionals' work practices, which includes both new challenges and opportunities. It also demonstrates how, today, there is still a disparity globally in amount of accessible resources online about art and culture. This subsequently has impacted the field by presenting a new perspective from Vietnam. It is important to shed light on Vietnam's route to and through digital transition and digitization of culture because it can allow them to make culture accessible online. This reflects the fact that artists and cultural professionals understand the importance in publishing contemporary art rather than using digitization for only preservation and archiving – highlighting the value they now place on this digitization process. Their mission includes showing contemporary Vietnamese life, the city, and work through sharing their work practices on social media. By showing the diversity in contemporary Vietnamese art through digitizing more artwork and displaying this content on social media sites. This shows that this process towards digitization is not just about digitizing everything or digitizing randomly selected artworks. In fact, there is purpose, choice, and a message in the digitization process. It is also a process and practice that is culture itself too. It relates to the local values and stories, myths and cultural icons of Vietnamese culture. It also places Vietnam in a regional context of South East Asia and to other developing countries and its cultural professionals as well as a global context by highlighting how countries experience digitization of culture in distinct ways. It has provided a novel contribution to the field by bringing different perspectives together, from artists, non-profit art organizations, museums, and art school directors.

Notes

1 For instance, Nualart (2016) writes about the presence of queer art in Vietnam. "In this exhibition, [representations of] men appeared all over the place", he says (personal communication, 2016). Later that year, Tan did an exhibition in Ho Chi Minh City (HCMC) that showed images of erect penises. The artist thinks this imagery is what drove the authorities to start closely monitoring his work, a surveillance that resulted in disquieting censorship the following year (personal communication, 2016). Eighteen of Tan's artworks were taken down from the *Cultural Collision* exhibition in Red River (Fleuve Rouge) gallery, Hanoi (Chiu and Genocchio 1996; Huynh 2005). Promadhattavedi (1996, 36) has observed that Tan's homoerotic artwork is better received in the West than in a society like Vietnam that frowns on individualism, although in "any country Truong Tan's work would be daring". Censorship has been mentioned in this discussion regularly, and almost as rhythmically has affected Tan and Himiko over their careers (Naziree 2010; NCAC

2007). Ngo Dinh Truc's urban intervention could avoid permit requests, because only conventional exhibitions in a venue open to the public need the licence from the Ministry of Information and Culture. Permission is required to hold any exhibition in a physical premises.

2 The Vietnam government filters and blocks certain content online. Two types of filtering seem to be employed by the two largest ISPs, VNPT and FPT. FPT deletes the [Domain Name System server] DNS record for the prohibited site and you simply cannot find it, while the VNPT system issues a notice of a blocked page. Vietnam Government websites, (2008), Retrieved July 20 from http://www.vnn.vn. The official search engine: http://www.search.com.vn Vietnam Ministry of Posts and Telecommunications Website: http://www.vnpt.com.vn.

References

Chiu, M., and B. Genocchio. (1996) A Silencing Sexuality. *Third Text* 10 (37): 87–90. https://doi.org/10.1080/09528829608576644

Duester, E. (2021) "Calls from Professionals for a 'Digital Culture Policy' in Vietnam." *Kyoto Review of South East Asia* 31 (1). https://kyotoreview.org/issue-31/calls-from-professionals-for-a-digital-culture-policy-in-vietnam/

Huynh, B. T. (2005) "Vietnamese Aesthetics from 1925 Onwards." PhD, University of Sydney. http://ses.library.usyd.edu.au/handle/2123/633.

Naziree, S. (2010) *How to Be and Angel.* Bangkok: Thavibu Gallery.

NCAC. (2007) Closer (Photographic exhibition). Online publication. http://wiki.ncac.org/Closer_(photographic_exhibition)

Nualart, C. (2016) "Queer Art in Vietnam: From Closet to Pride in Two Decades." *Palgrave Commun* 2: 16009. https://doi.org/10.1057/palcomms.2016.9

Promadhattavedi, C. (1996) "Twenty Vietnamese painters: Aspects of contemporary Vietnamese painting." In *Cultural Representation in Transition: New Vietnamese Painting* (pp. 32–37). Bangkok: The Siam Society.

Index